The New York Coffee Guide.
2012

Edited by
Jeffrey Young
and Emma Meltzer

Author: Allegra Strategies

Photography: Margot Mausner

Design: John Osborne

Website: Lee Goldsmith
and Tim Spring

Other content: Sally Conor, Maximilian
Gower, Jeremy Hersh and Kate Meltzer

Publisher: Allegra Publications Ltd

Allegra
PUBLICATIONS

Published in 2012 by Allegra Publications Ltd No.1 Northumberland Ave, Trafalgar Square, London, WC2N 5BW

Visit our website:
www.newyorkcoffeeguide.com

All information was accurate at time of going to press.

Published by *Allegra* PUBLICATIONS Ltd © 2012
No.1 Northumberland Ave, Trafalgar Square, London, WC2N 5BW

Foreword

It is an honor to be asked to write the foreword to The New York Coffee Guide. Both the city and the beverage have shaped my own story.

I grew up in the borough of Brooklyn, in the poor, red brick projects of Canarsie. It was the kind of place where fathers like mine tried to hold down one blue-collar job after another, and kids like me played ball on the asphalt schoolyards. The idea of pursuing the American Dream was not dead where I grew up, but for many it seemed elusive.

Although a college football scholarship was my ticket out, my own dream to build a better life for myself and my family took off years later - because of coffee.

I was on a business trip to Milan when I wandered into an Italian espresso bar and discovered what I still believe is coffee's most addictive power: the sense of community created by a perfectly crafted beverage and enjoyed in a familial café.

This was the very experience I aspired to recreate across the US back in the late 1980s.

Not until these past two decades has coffee's connective ability reached so many corners in America. And perhaps nowhere else in the country is this phenomenon more concentrated than in the multicultural neighborhoods and crowded avenues of New York City. For decades, coffee here was predominantly consumed for its caffeine, not savored for its flavors, and sipped under the florescent lights of all-night diners or gulped on the run after being picked up from sidewalk carts or vending machines.

Today, New York City has established a modern coffee culture that honors as well as rivals its European counterparts. A rich variety of establishments, from independent artisans to local Starbucks stores, source the finest coffee beans from the far reaches of the world and bring them to neighborhoods not far from where I grew up: Williamsburg, Greenpoint and Park Slope etc. More importantly, however, is the vital flavor of community that the city's cafés are helping preserve as well as foster. This blend of craftsmanship and human connection is defining New York's coffee culture, which at no time has been more vibrant.

In a city famously known for having millions of stories, New York City remains a place where lives do not just begin, but are launched. The city challenges everyone it touches - natives, new residents, aspiring artists, ambitious entrepreneurs, weekend tourists - to follow their dreams, be it opening a corner business or building a global brand.

Like a truly delicious cup of coffee, New York City is complex, but it still has the potential to inspire greatness in all of us.

Howard Schultz
CEO, President and Chairman,
Starbucks Coffee Company

Contents

Introduction

Welcome to The New York Coffee Guide 2012 – the definitive guide to New York's best coffee venues.

The New York Coffee Guide was born out of a quest to discover great places to go for coffee in New York. This great city has a long, rich coffee house tradition and now is home to a thriving independent coffee scene, meaning both locals and visitors are spoilt for choice.

We have compiled The New York Coffee Guide to assist and inform those who are willing to travel all throughout the boroughs of New York in the hunt for great coffee experiences. It might be the coffee itself that is the main

attraction, or perhaps the excitement of visiting a new and unique coffee shop. Our aim is to encourage fellow coffee lovers to try something different and discover places they otherwise may never have known existed.

Allegra Strategies is an established leader in research and business intelligence for the coffee industry. We have drawn on this research as well as a variety of other sources to compile The New York Coffee Guide.

About the Guide

Every venue that appears in The New York Coffee Guide has been visited and rated by our expert team. The ratings fall into two distinct categories: coffee rating and overall rating.

RATING.

COFFEE 4.50 / 5

OVERALL 4.50 / 5

Coffee rating

The coffee rating is not only about the taste of the coffee - it also takes into account numerous other coffee credentials such as the coffee roaster, equipment used, barista skills, visual appeal of the coffee and several other factors that demonstrate the venue's overall attitude to coffee.

The following question is the guiding principle used to determine the coffee ratings: To what extent does this coffee venue deliver an amazing coffee experience?

Overall rating

In combination with the coffee experience, this rating also considers to what extent the coffee shop experience delivers a "wow" factor to the customer. Elements that are taken into account include store environment, ambience, design, customer service and food quality, among other factors.

To determine a coffee shop's overall rating the following question is used

as the guiding principle: How do the combination of coffee and the coffee shop experience translate to exceptional levels of customer excitement?

Symbols used throughout The New York Coffee Guide

 Pourover / single source drip available

 Decaffeinated coffee available

 Coffee beans sold on site

 Gluten-free products available

 Venue has a loyalty card

 Soy milk available

 Toilets

 Parent & baby friendly

 Disabled access

 Credit cards accepted

 Wifi available

 Computer friendly

Licensed

The right cup gets you noticed.

A Brief History of Coffee in New York

The early years

800 AD The coffee plant (Coffea) attracts human interest and consumption as early as 800 AD in the Kaffe region of Ethiopia. According to legend, it was an Ethiopian goat herder named Kaldi who first discovered how animated his herd of goats became after chewing on the red berries.

13th – 16th centuries

Coffee berries are brought to the Arabian Peninsula and the first known cultivation of coffee is established in the area known today as Yemen. A crude version of coffee - roasted beans crushed and boiled in water - is developed and by 1475 coffee houses are established in Constantinople, Cairo and throughout Persia.

17th and 18th centuries

Travelers to the Arabian Peninsula bring coffee to Europe and Britain. Coffee houses are established as centers for the exchange of ideas and information, as well as forums for debate.

1650 The first English coffee house is established in Oxford by a Jewish gentleman named Jacob at the Angel in the parish of St Peter.

1668 Coffee is brought to New Amsterdam (Old New York) by Dutch settlers.

1696 Built in the style of the coffee houses of Europe, The King's Arms is the first coffee house established in New York.

1732 The Exchange Coffee House is opened on Broadway and establishes itself as a center for commerce.

1750 The Exchange Coffee House loses favor and is replaced by The Merchants Coffee House (on what is now known as Wall Street), which grows to be the foremost gathering place in the city for trade and political debate.

1765 A warning to the citizens of New York to end their rioting against the Stamp Act is read at The Merchants Coffee House.

1773 The Boston Tea Party, a revolt against the high taxation levied by King George III on tea imported to the New World, sees coffee replace tea as the drink of choice in the colonies.

1784 The Bank of New York, the oldest bank in the country, is founded at The Merchants Coffee House.

1792 The New York Stock Exchange is established at the Tontine Coffee House on Wall Street, where the first public stocks are sold.

19th and 20th centuries

With the rise of industrialization and technological advances, coffee drinking becomes accessible to everyone, not just the elite. People begin drinking it more in their homes and the demand for the beans rises, leading to rapid growth in coffee production.

1840 The Gillies Coffee Company is founded in New York, a company that survives as the oldest coffee merchant in the city.

1850 Folgers Coffee is founded in San Francisco.

1864 The first commercial coffee roasting machine, Jabez Burns' #1 Coffee Roaster, receives a US patent.

1882 The Coffee Exchange of New York begins regulating the coffee trade, setting standards for the traffic of the commodity as well as the quality of the product.

1892 Maxwell House Coffee is founded.

1907 Porto Rico Importing Company opens on Bleecker Street.

1911 The National Coffee Association of the USA is established, the first trade association for the US coffee industry.

1920s As Prohibition takes effect, national coffee sales flourish.

1927 Caffe Reggio opens in Greenwich Village with the first espresso machine in New York.

1946 Coffee consumption in the US hits an all-time high, reaching 19.8 pounds per person per annum, twice what it was in 1900.

1950s / 1960s After WWII, the importation of coffee is impeded. The Pan American Coffee Bureau is established to promote the drinking of coffee and assist its production in Central America. One such promotion is the popularization of the "coffee break".

Italian-style cafés serving espresso and pastries begin to pop up in Greenwich Village and Little Italy. These coffee shops become creative and intellectual centers for artists, writers, musicians, and intellectuals.

1971 Starbucks opens its first store at Pike Place Market in Seattle, Washington.

1982 The Specialty Coffee Association of America (SCAA) is founded.

Late 1980s

After an inspiring visit to Italy, Howard Schultz buys Starbucks and revamps the brand.

1994 La Colombe Torrefaction is established in Philadelphia and pioneers the concept of "culinary coffee".

Manhattan's first Starbucks store opens on the Upper West Side at 86th Street and Broadway.

1995 Intelligentsia Coffee & Tea opens in Chicago and grows to become one of the major names in the American coffee industry.

1999 Stumptown Coffee Roasters opens in Portland, Oregon.

The Cup of Excellence is established.

Last decade

The 2000s see specialty coffee and the third-wave coffee movement emerge in the US, starting in Portland and Seattle and spreading to California, New York and beyond. This movement focuses on ethical trading, coffee freshness and new roasting techniques.

2000 The first World Barista Championship takes place in Monte Carlo.

2001 Ninth Street Espresso opens in Alphabet City.

2003 Gorilla Coffee opens in Park Slope, Brooklyn.

2005 Café Grumpy opens with its own roastery in Greenpoint, Brooklyn.

2007 La Colombe Torrefaction opens its first New York outpost in Tribeca.

2009 Stumptown Coffee opens its first New York location at The Ace Hotel in Brooklyn.

2010 The Blue Bottle Coffee Company opens its roastery in a converted warehouse in Williamsburg, Brooklyn.

American Michael Phillips wins the World Barista Championship in London, United Kingdom.

2012 Australian-owned Toby's Estate opens in Williamsburg, Brooklyn.

The first New York Coffee Guide is published.

COFFEE VENUES KEY

Lower Manhattan

East Village & Lower East Side

Greenwich Village & Neighboring

Midtown & Gramercy

Lower Manhattan

Lower Manhattan is a diverse and exciting area with a variety of different identities. The business-savvy Financial District has the hustle and bustle of Wall Street at its heart, while trendy Tribeca is a cool, popular neighborhood that overlooks the Hudson River. By night, the Meatpacking District and the larger West Village are immensely fashionable, with great shopping options, chic restaurants and popular bars and clubs.

Cafe Angelique

49 Grove Street, Manhattan, NY 10014 | West Village ·····································

OPEN.

Mon-Fri.	7:00am - 10:00pm
Sat-Sun.	7:00am - 11:00pm

This café for the fashionable set is situated in the chic West Village. Shaped by the owner's roots, this Israeli-inspired, European-style shop offers such delights as fresh salads, sandwiches and a menu full of pastries and baked goods, not to mention some super Italian espresso, courtesy of imported Lavazza beans. The café is elegant and charming, perched on a cobblestoned corner, and offers some of the best people-watching in the city. Angelique is a great weekend spot to grab a bite or take a cup to go as an accompaniment for a stroll around the neighborhood.

FOOD.

A full menu of breakfast offerings, sandwiches, salads, baked goods and pastries, some from Cafe Angelique's Bleecker Street location, others from neighborhood bakeries or imported from Israel.

CONTACT.

(212) 414-1400
www.cafeangelique.com
info@cafeangelique.com
Subway 1 (Christopher St - Sheridan Sq)

OVERVIEW.

Category
Multi-independent
Owner
Isaac Ben-Avraham
First opened
2002

COFFEE & EQUIPMENT.

Roaster
Lavazza
Machine
La Cimbali, 3 groups
Grinder
La Cimbali
Bulk brewer
Fetco

PRICES.

Filter / Drip	$1.85
Espresso	$2.00
Cappuccino	$3.80
Latte	$3.80

Other locations
Bleecker Street / Prince Street /
New Jersey

RATING.

COFFEE	
3.75 / 5	🫘🫘🫘🫘🫘
OVERALL	
4.00 / 5	★★★★☆

Cafe Cluny

284 West 12th Street, Manhattan, NY 10014 | West Village ....

OPEN.

Mon.	8:00am - 11:00pm
Tue-Fri.	8:00am - midnight
Sat.	9:00am - midnight
Sun.	9:00am - 11:00pm

Tucked away on a sunny corner in the West Village is this delightful restaurant, which exudes elegance. Classic French style accents the menu, the restaurant interior and the uniforms of the staff who don nautical striped St. James shirts. There has been a movement in New York recently to improve the quality of restaurant coffee, and Cafe Cluny is definitely participating in this shift. Traditional European espresso is served with grace along with beautifully prepared meals, and brunch at this café is a particularly fabulous treat.

FOOD.

The French-inspired menu includes breakfast, lunch and dinner with brunch on the weekends. Baked goods are from Amy's Bread while granola and chocolate bars are made on site.

CONTACT.

(212) 255-6900
www.cafecluny.com
info@cafecluny.com
Subway A, C, E, L (14th St - 8th Ave) or 1 (Christopher St) or 1, 2, 3, F, M, L (14th St - 6th Ave)

OVERVIEW.

Category
Independent
Owner
Steven Abrowitz, Lynn Wagenknecht and Judi Wong
First opened
2007

COFFEE & EQUIPMENT.

Roaster
La Colombe Torrefaction
Machine
La Spaziale, 2 groups
Grinder
La Spaziale Astro
Bulk brewer
Bunn

PRICES.

Filter / Drip	$4.00
Espresso	$3.50
Cappuccino	$4.50
Latte	$4.50

RATING.

COFFEE 3.50 / 5	
OVERALL 4.00 / 5	

Cafe Minerva

302 West 4th Street, Manhattan, NY 10014 | **West Village** ....

Cafe Minerva is another West Village restaurant with a decidedly European feel. Enormous front windows give the interior a beautiful glow that only natural light can lend. Small tables surround a center bar with the counter space dominated by a beautiful Victoria Arduino Athena espresso machine. The focal point of the bar, the Athena presides over the entire café with an air of regal authority. Feel welcome to linger here for a few hours over your coffee and order some small plates, which offer welcome sustenance after an afternoon of daydreaming.

OPEN.

Mon-Fri.	7:00am - 11:00pm
Sat-Sun.	7:00am - midnight

OVERVIEW.

Category
Independent
Owner
Matthew Paratore
First opened
2010

COFFEE & EQUIPMENT.

Roaster
Red House Roasters, Dallis Bros Coffee and Cafe D'arte
Machine
Victoria Arduino Athena
Grinder
Nuova Simonelli MDX

PRICES.

Filter / Drip	$2.25
Espresso	$2.50
Cappuccino	$3.50
Latte	$3.80

FOOD.

A full Italian-inspired menu with sweet and savory breakfast items in the morning, freshly made baked goods, paninis, salads and large and small plates throughout the day.

CONTACT.

(212) 242-4800
Subway A, C, E, L (8th Ave) or 1 (Christopher St) or 1, 2, 3, F, V, L (14th St - 6th Ave)

RATING.

COFFEE	4.00 / 5	🫘 🫘 🫘 🫘 🫘
OVERALL	4.25 / 5	★ ★ ★ ★ ✬

Fika

66 Pearl Street, Manhattan, NY 10004 | **Financial District** ....

OPEN.
Mon-Fri.	7:00am - 7:00pm
Sat.	9:00am - 4:00pm
Sun.	10:00am - 4:00pm

With a space that's somewhere between antique and modern, this bright café offers a pleasant respite from the intensity of Wall Street. The coffee is Swedish style (as is the café as a whole) with medium-roasted beans creating a coffee that is sweet and mild. The café's front patio is available when the weather permits and is a lovely spot to watch impeccably dressed businessmen go by while enjoying an espresso and maybe a chocolate or pastry made by Fika's own team. In Swedish "fika" is a verb meaning to take a coffee break, so take the cue and enjoy exactly that at this chic spot.

FOOD.
A menu with offerings such as fresh sandwiches and salads, as well as baked goods and chocolates all prepared by Fika's team of chefs.

CONTACT.
(646) 837-6588
www.fikanyc.com
Subway N, R (Whitehall St) or 1 (South Ferry) or 4, 5 (Bowling Green)

OVERVIEW.
Category
Multi-independent
Owner
Lars Akerlund and David Johansson
First opened
2010

COFFEE & EQUIPMENT.
Roaster
Löfbergs Lila
Machine
Synesso
Grinder
Mazzer
Bulk brewer
Bunn

PRICES.
Filter / Drip	$2.00
Espresso	$2.00
Cappuccino	$3.50
Latte	$3.75

Other locations
West 58th Street / Park Avenue South

RATING.

COFFEE 4.25 / 5	🫘 🫘 🫘 🫘 🫘
OVERALL 4.25 / 5	★ ★ ★ ★ ✩

Jack's

138 West 10th Street, Manhattan, NY 10014 | West Village ....

OPEN.

Mon-Sat.	7:00am - 8:00pm
Sun.	8:00am - 8:00pm

This cozy West Village café is more than just a coffee shop - it's a nostalgic snapshot of New York life. Much like the photographs that owner Jack has taken of the neighborhood and locals, Jack's reflects the quiet side of the city that so often gets lost in the rush of everyday life. Indulge in one of Jack's incredible chocolate chip cookies, made from his aunt's secret recipe, and pair it with a cup of splendidly balanced stir-brewed coffee. Jack's is a place to come and feel good, take an hour out of your day and simply enjoy.

OVERVIEW.
Category
Chain
Owner
Jack Mazzola
First opened
2003

COFFEE & EQUIPMENT.
Roaster
Jack's Stir Brew Roast
Machine
La Marzocco GB/5
Grinder
Mazzer
Bulk brewer
Jack's Stir Brewer

FOOD.
An assortment of baked goods, including chocolate cookies made using a family recipe.

PRICES.

Filter / Drip	$2.25
Espresso	$2.25
Cappuccino	$3.75
Latte	$3.75

Other locations
222 Front Street / Amagansett

CONTACT.
(212) 929-0821
www.jacksstirbrew.com
info@jacksstirbrew.com
Subway A, B, C, D, E, F, M (W. 4th St)
and 1 (Christopher St - Sheridan Sq)

Jack's Stir Brewer is a patented system that stirs the coffee continually while it brews

RATING.

COFFEE
4.00 / 5

OVERALL
4.00 / 5

Joe West Village

141 Waverly Place, Manhattan, NY 10014 | **West Village** ....

This New York institution has been around for close to a decade and continues to grow, with its newest location on the Upper East Side. Joe exemplifies the social centers that coffee houses can be - people come here on lazy weekend mornings to meet, talk and work, while lines usually go out the door during peak hours. Joe offers a drip bar in the afternoon with a rotating menu of single origins and its espresso levels well in milk drinks. Of all the Joe cafés across the city, this location is particularly charming and has a knack for attracting local celebrities.

OPEN.

Mon-Fri.	7:00am - 8:00pm
Sat-Sun.	8:00am - 8:00pm

OVERVIEW.

Category
Chain
Owner
Jonathan and Gabrielle Rubinstein
First opened
2003

COFFEE & EQUIPMENT.

Roaster
Ecco Coffee
Machine
La Marzocco GB/5
Grinder
Mazzer Robur E
Bulk brewer
Fetco

Other locations
Seven other locations in New York

PRICES.

Filter / Drip	$2.25
Espresso	$2.50
Cappuccino	$3.75
Latte	$3.75

FOOD.

An assortment of cookies, muffins and other baked goods from Erica's Rugelach and Ceci Cela. Housemade baked goods are also made in partnership with Ovenly.

CONTACT.

(212) 924-6750
www.joenewyork.com
joecoffeestore@gmail.com
Subway A, C, E, B, D, F, M (W. 4th St) or 1, 2 (Christopher St)

RATING.

COFFEE	
4.25 / 5	🌰 🌰 🌰 🌰 🌰
OVERALL	
4.50 / 5	★ ★ ★ ★ ✬

Kaffe 1668

275 Greenwich Street, Manhattan, NY 10007 | **Tribeca** ....

This café has everything the hungry worker could possibly ask for, offering wifi, outlets and a nice communal table in the bright front area, but this cool Tribeca spot is just as awesome as a hangout, with its interesting industrial yet homey vibe. The food is fresh and the coffee is some of the best in the city - Kaffe 1668 explores the best coffees of any given season and offers one of the most varied coffee menus around. All drip coffee is brewed to order on a Clover machine and around six different single origins are available at any one time.

The space is deceptively large, with additional seating downstairs, and a quirky sheep motif is a nod to coffee's folkloric origins.

OPEN.

Mon-Fri.	6:30am - 10:00pm
Sat-Sun.	7:30am - 10:00pm

OVERVIEW.

Category
Independent
Owner
Mikael Tjarnberg and
Thomas Tjarnberg
First opened
2008

COFFEE & EQUIPMENT.

Roaster
Counter Culture, Intelligentsia, Ecco
Caffe, Plowshares and Toby's Estate
Machine
Synesso
Grinder
Mazzer Robur E
Bulk brewer
Clover

PRICES.

Filter / Drip	$2.76
Espresso	$2.53
Cappuccino	$3.91
Latte	$4.14

FOOD.

Sandwiches, baked goods and sweets
all made fresh in the café.

CONTACT.

(212) 693-3750
www.kaffe1668.com
kaffe1668@gmail.com
Subway 1, 2, 3 (Chambers St)

RATING.

COFFEE	4.50 / 5	🫘🫘🫘🫘🫘
OVERALL	4.50 / 5	★★★★⯪

Kava Cafe

803 Washington Street, Manhattan, NY 10014 | **The Meatpacking District** ....

It's all about the look at this polished coffee bar, where even the baristas are dressed to the nines. Decked out in fedoras and skinny black ties, these stylish coffee slingers run a drip bar and pull excellent shots on their sleek La Marzocco Strada MP. The interior is designed in the fashion of a typical Italian coffee bar, with a standing area where customers can sip espresso, but if you're looking to relax for a while, walk through to the beautiful garden patio.

OPEN.

Mon-Fri.	7:00am - 8:00pm
Sat-Sun.	8:00am - 9:00pm

OVERVIEW.

Category
Independent
Owner
John Saric
First opened
2011

COFFEE & EQUIPMENT.

Roaster
Ceremony Roasters
Machine
La Marzocco Strada MP
Grinder
Mazzer Robur E, Mazzer Super Jolly
Bulk brewer
Fetco

PRICES.

Filter / Drip	$1.84
Espresso	$2.76
Cappuccino	$3.50
Latte	$3.50

FOOD.

Fresh salads and sandwiches are available, as is gelato, beer on tap and baked goods from Balthazar and Brooklyn Bridge Bakery.

CONTACT.

(212) 255-7495
www.kavanyc.com
info@kavanyc.com
Subway L (8th Ave) or A, C, E (14th St)

RATING.

COFFEE
4.25 / 5

OVERALL
4.00 / 5

La Colombe Torrefaction Tribeca

319 Church Street, Manhattan, NY 10013 | **Tribeca** ·····································

This was the first New York home for respected Philadelphia roaster La Colombe and has since become a city favorite, with two more locations along Lafayette Street. Hugging the corner of a historic Tribeca building, this spot has a quiet, stately personality, with plenty of light streaming in through the expansive windows. The signature streamlined elegance of La Colombe's other venues is also present here, with handmade cups, a polished wooden interior and twin Faema E61 espresso machines all making an appearance. This Tribeca location is the mama bear of the La Colombe New York family – smaller than the Noho shop, but bigger than the Soho location – and is a stylish spot to enjoy some of the best coffee in the city.

OPEN.

Mon-Fri.	7:30am - 6:30pm
Sat-Sun.	8:30am - 6:30pm

OVERVIEW.

Category
Chain
Owner
Jean Philippe Iberti, Todd Carmichael
and Doug Wolfe
First opened
2007

COFFEE & EQUIPMENT.

Roaster
La Colombe Torrefaction
Machine
Faema E61
Grinder
Mazzer
Bulk brewer
Fetco

Other locations
400 Lafayette Street / 270 Lafayette
Street / Philadelphia / Chicago / Seoul,
South Korea

PRICES.

Filter / Drip	$2.00
Espresso	$2.00
Cappuccino	$3.50
Latte	$3.50

FOOD.

Baked goods such as pastries from
Payard and olive oil cake from
Kate's Cakes.

CONTACT.

(212) 343-1515
www.lacolombe.com
generalcontact@lacolombe.net
Subway A, C, E (Canal St) or N, R
(Canal St) or 1 (Franklin St)

RATING.

COFFEE	4.75 / 5	🫘 🫘 🫘 🫘 🫘
OVERALL	4.50 / 5	★ ★ ★ ★ ½

O Cafe

482 6th Avenue, Manhattan, NY 10012 | West Village ....

OPEN.

Mon-Sat.	7:00am - 8:30pm
Sun.	8:00am - 8:00pm

A gem amidst the gray, shoe-repair-shop-littered northern stretch of the West Village, O Cafe is serious but thankfully unpretentious. On a sunny day, it feels like California; the Brazilian-sourced, Florida-roasted espresso is strong, the rotating pourover options are excellent and well priced, and the baristas are warm and friendly. Argentinian owner Fernando Aciar's interest in Brazil extends beyond the coffee - several items on the expansive food menu have Brazilian roots, including the delicious gluten-free pao de quejo (cheese balls). In addition to several chocolate-inflected beverages on the menu, O makes its own delectable chocolate bars (also Brazilian sourced). O Cafe is a great argument for the notion that the West Village extends to 14th Street.

CONTACT.

(212) 229-2233
www.ocafeny.com
ocafe@ocafeny.com
Subway F, M and L (14th St- 6th Ave)

OVERVIEW.

Category
Independent
Owner
Fernando Aciar
First opened
2011

COFFEE & EQUIPMENT.

Roaster
Panther Coffee
Machine
La Marzocco Strada
Grinder
Mazzer

PRICES.

Filter / Drip	$1.75
Espresso	$2.55
Cappuccino	$3.60
Latte	$3.90

FOOD.

A menu of Brazilian-inspired sweet and savory treats, sandwiches and some seriously tempting housemade chocolate bars.

RATING.

COFFEE 4.25 / 5	OVERALL 4.25 / 5

Prodigy Coffee

33 Carmine Street, Manhattan, NY 10014 | West Village ....

OPEN.

Mon-Fri.	7:00am - 8:00pm
Sat.	8:00am - 8:00pm
Sun.	8:00am - 7:00pm

Prodigy Coffee is a welcome addition to the growing West Village coffee scene. The shop has some serious pedigree, with owners who have been in the coffee and café industries for the past 30 years. Chris Calkins was involved with Starbucks, Peet's and Spinelli Coffee Company before returning home to join forces with Ira Horowitz and open this lovely shop, which serves premium coffee in a sleek and comfortable environment. Coffee is an art here, and the menu is updated seasonally with new blends and single origins custom roasted for the shop. Try the Prodigy Coffee Snake Bite: a double shot of espresso in dark chocolate.

FOOD.

A small selection of baked goods from Newman's, Green & Ackerman and Mille-feuille Patisserie.

CONTACT.

(212) 414-4142
www.prodigycoffee.com
info@prodigycoffee.com
Subway 1 (Christopher St - Sheridan Sq) or A, C, E, B, D, F, M (W. 4th St)

OVERVIEW.

Category
Independent
Owner
Chris Calkins and Ira Horowitz
First opened
January 2012

COFFEE & EQUIPMENT.

Roaster
House roast by George Howell Coffee Company
Machine
La Marzocco Linea, 2 groups
Grinder
Mazzer Robur E, Mazzer
Bulk brewer
Curtis

PRICES.

Filter / Drip	$2.25
Espresso	$2.75
Cappuccino	$3.50
Latte	$4.00

RATING.

COFFEE	4.00 / 5	🫘 🫘 🫘 🫘 🫘
OVERALL	4.00 / 5	★ ★ ★ ★ ★

Sant Ambroeus

259 West 4th Street, Manhattan, NY 10014 | West Village ·······························

OPEN.
Mon-Sun.   9:00am - 11:00pm

Tucked away on a little corner of the West Village, this small restaurant has a European sensibility that fits perfectly with the neighborhood's narrow, grid-defying streets. Indeed, Sant Ambroeus has the feel of a quintessential Italian café and the coffee certainly supports that impression. Order an espresso here and you'll be served the most delightfully smooth shot this side of the Atlantic. On a warm day, sit outside and watch the neighborhood locals and Magnolia Bakery-seeking tourists pass by.

FOOD.
A full menu of Italian fare, with pastries and full plates in the morning for breakfast, as well as full service lunch and dinner throughout the day.

CONTACT.
(212) 604-9254
www.santambroeus.com
Subway 1, 2 (Christopher St - Sheridan Sq) or A, C, E, B, D, F, M (W. 4th St)

OVERVIEW.
Category
Multi-independent
Owner
Dimitri Pauli and Gherardo Guarducci
First opened
2005

COFFEE & EQUIPMENT.
Roaster
Lavazza
Machine
La Cimbali, 3 groups
Grinder
Mazzer

PRICES.
Filter / Drip	Americano: $4.00
Espresso	$4.00
Cappuccino	$5.00
Latte	$5.00

Other locations
Madison Avenue / Main Street, Southampton

RATING.

COFFEE
4.00 / 5

OVERALL
4.00 / 5

East Village & Lower East Side

The East Village and surrounding areas all have a laidback, colorful vibe. Tompkins Square Park in Alphabet City and the range of vibrant off-Broadway theatres in the East Village are worth a visit, while the Lower East Side is packed with trendy shops, vintage stores, contemporary art galleries and rich local history. The neighborhood still retains much of its Jewish heritage in the buildings, restaurants and synagogues that were established by immigrant communities during the 20th century.

Abraço

86 East 7th Street, Manhattan, NY 10003 | **East Village** ....

 At Abraço, simplicity rules. A lack of tables or chairs makes this a coffee bar in the most literal sense and it is also one of the city's best. The menu at this compact East Village shop is uncomplicated - no decaf, no soy milk, no bulk brewer - and the simple combination of exceptional espresso drinks, freshly ground and brewed coffee from the drip bar, housemade pastries and small plates all reflect the care and attention to detail that characterize Abraço. Pure, simple and utterly delicious.

PRICES.

Filter / Drip	$2.50
Espresso	$2.00
Cappuccino	$3.50
Latte	$4.00

FOOD.

Fresh gourmet sweet and savory
selections, the variety of which
changes depending on the season.

CONTACT.

www.abraconyc.com
info@abraconyc.com
Subway 4, 6 (Astor Place)

OPEN.

Mon.	Closed
Tue-Sat.	8:00am - 4:00pm
Sun.	9:00am - 4:00pm

OVERVIEW.

Category
Independent
Owner
Jamie McCormick
and Elizabeth Quijada
First opened
2007

COFFEE & EQUIPMENT.

Roaster
Counter Culture
Machine
La Marzocco Linea, 2 groups
Grinder
Mazzer

RATING.

COFFEE 4.75 / 5	🫘🫘🫘🫘🫘
OVERALL 4.25 / 5	★★★★⯪

East Village & Lower East Side

Au Breve

51 Cooper Square, Manhattan, NY 10003 | **Greenwich Village** ....

Tucked away inside the Cooper Union building, Au Breve is a hidden bastion of coffee excellence. The baristas here are fanatical and the constantly rotating espresso menu is always worth a look. Most customers take their coffee to go en route to class or business in the East Village, but if you have the time, buck that trend and stay for a pourover - just ask your barista for a recommendation.

OPEN.

Mon-Thu.	7:30am - 8:00pm
Fri.	7:30am - 6:00pm
Sat.	Closed
Sun.	8:30am - 8:00pm

OVERVIEW.

Category
Independent
Owner
Eddie Klaynberg, Daniel Klaynberg
and Eric Brody
First opened
2011

COFFEE & EQUIPMENT.

Roaster
Dallis Bros Coffee
Machine
La Marzocco Linea MP, 2 groups
Grinder
Mazzer Robur E, Ditting
Bulk brewer
Fetco 2052 E

PRICES.

Filter / Drip	$2.00
Espresso	$2.50
Cappuccino	$3.75
Latte	$4.00

FOOD.

Pastries from kosher bakery, My Most
Favorite Food.

CONTACT.

www.aubreve.com
info@aubreve.com
Subway 6 (Astor Place), or N, R
(8th Street-NYU)

RATING.

COFFEE	
4.25 / 5	🫘🫘🫘🫘🫘
OVERALL	
4.25 / 5	★★★★⯪

Bluebird Coffee Shop

71 East 1st Street, Manhattan, NY 10003 | **East Village** ....

OPEN.

Mon-Sat.	8:00am - 7:00pm
Sun.	9:00am - 7:00pm

Although not much space is to be found at this compact East Village spot, the coffee more than makes up for the cramped quarters. Counter Culture beans supply this charming coffee bar, while sandwiches and granola are freshly prepared in house. During the summer, this café is particularly lovely, as the windows are thrown open, the sun shines in and locals stop by to chat with the baristas, creating a cool, calm vibe.

FOOD.

Pastries supplied by Colson Patisserie in Brooklyn, with freshly prepared sandwiches during the afternoon, housemade granola, yogurt and other sweets throughout the day.

CONTACT.

(212) 260-1879
www.bluebirdcoffeeshop.com
bluebirdcoffeeshop@gmail.com
Subway F (Second Ave)

OVERVIEW.

Category
Independent
Owner
Alex Hall and Sabrina Godfrey
First opened
2009

COFFEE & EQUIPMENT.

Roaster
Counter Culture
Machine
La Marzocco FB/80, 2 groups
Grinder
Mazzer
Bulk brewer
Fetco

PRICES.

Filter / Drip	$1.75
Espresso	$2.50
Cappuccino	$3.75
Latte	$4.00

RATING.

COFFEE 4.25 / 5	🫘🫘🫘🫘🫘
OVERALL 4.25 / 5	★★★★⯪

Bowery Coffee

89 East Houston Street, Manhattan, NY 10012 | Lower East Side ....

OPEN.
Mon-Sun.   7:00am - 7:00pm

Soho can be exhausting, so before embarking on a day of shopping or a night of debauchery, give yourself a moment at Bowery Coffee. Owner Gadi Galin used to sell vintage lamps in this space (and still does in the basement), and his affinity for antiques is clear in his coffee shop. An old clock features prominently and the walls have been built using recycled timber from Scranton, Pennsylvania. Although there are only a few small tables, high ceilings give the space an open, airy feel. Bowery baristas are careful and amiable, and the Counter Culture beans on offer are top-notch, with a drip that is a delight: rich and not overly acidic.

FOOD.

Pastries from Balthazar and doughnuts from The Doughnut Plant.

CONTACT.

(212) 966-5162
bowerycoffee@gmail.com
Subway F (Delancey St)

OVERVIEW.

Category
Independent
Owner
Gadi Galin
First opened
2011

COFFEE & EQUIPMENT.

Roaster
Counter Culture
Machine
La Marzocco Strada MP
Grinder
Mazzer Major
Bulk brewer
Fetco

PRICES.

Filter / Drip	$2.25
Espresso	$2.75
Cappuccino	$3.75
Latte	$4.25

RATING.

COFFEE 4.00 / 5	🌰 🌰 🌰 🌰 🌰
OVERALL 4.00 / 5	★ ★ ★ ★ ★

Everyman Espresso

136 East 13th Street, Manhattan, NY 10003 | **East Village** ....

Everyman shares its space with the lobby of the Classic Stage Company theater, but to say that it's the best theater-lobby coffee you've ever had would not do this place justice. This is a serious coffee shop in its own right; the fact that Meryl Streep might brush past your table on her way into the theater is merely a pleasant side effect. Everyman baristas are fanatical, expert and approachable and their single-origin pourovers are worth the wait, while the Counter Culture espresso is smooth and reliable. Whether to take your espresso straight and experience its nuances head-on or order a flawless latte can turn out to be quite the Sophie's Choice.

OPEN.

Mon-Fri.	7:00am - 8:00pm
Sat-Sun.	8:00am - 8:00pm

OVERVIEW.

Category
Independent
Owner
Sam Penix
First opened
2007

COFFEE & EQUIPMENT.

Roaster
Counter Culture
Machine
Synesso Cyncra, 2 groups
Grinder
Mazzer Robur E
Bulk brewer
Fetco

Other locations
Soho

PRICES.

Filter / Drip	$2.00
Espresso	$3.00
Cappuccino	$3.75
Latte	$4.25

FOOD.

A selection of pastries from Ceci Cela Bakery, Downtown Cookie Company and Whimsy & Spice Bakery.

CONTACT.

(212) 533-0524
www.everymanespresso.com
Subway L (Third Ave) or 4, 5, 6, N, Q, R, L (14th St - Union Sq)

RATING.

COFFEE 4.50 / 5

OVERALL 4.50 / 5

La Colombe Torrefaction East Village

400 Lafayette Street, Manhattan, NY 10003 | **East Village** ....

Every detail of this Philadelphia import is flawless. The space is beautiful and baristas hold court at the marble-topped wraparound bar, which serves as the focal point of this sun-drenched shop. Polished wooden tables inch along the windows and are perfect spots to relax with an expertly pulled espresso. La Colombe has a wonderfully calm and friendly atmosphere, thanks to the baristas, who work with ease and speed, making long lines fly quickly. The coffee is always exceptional, well-balanced, smooth and aromatic, whether on its own or in a milk drink. Even the tableware is exquisite: handcrafted cups and saucers are lovely reminders of the care that goes into everything here.

OPEN.

Mon-Fri.	7:30am - 6:30pm
Sat-Sun.	8:30am - 6:30pm

OVERVIEW.

Category
Chain
Owner
Jean Philippe Iberti, Todd Carmichael and Doug Wolfe
First opened
2011

COFFEE & EQUIPMENT.

Roaster
La Colombe Torrefaction
Machine
La Marzocco GB/5
Grinder
Mazzer Super Jolly
Bulk brewer
Fetco

Other locations
Soho / Tribeca

PRICES.

Filter / Drip	$2.00
Espresso	$2.00
Cappuccino	$3.50
Latte	$3.50

FOOD.

Baked goods such as pastries from Payard and olive oil cake from Kate's Cakes.

CONTACT.

(212) 677-5834
www.lacolombe.com
generalcontact@lacolombe.net
Subway 4, 6 (Astor Place), N, R (8th St - NYU)

East Village & Lower East Side

RATING.

COFFEE	4.75 / 5	🫘 🫘 🫘 🫘 🫘
OVERALL	4.75 / 5	★ ★ ★ ★ ★

Lost Weekend NYC

45 Orchard Street, Manhattan, NY 10002 | **Lower East Side** ....

The combination of gallery space, clothing store and coffee shop might seem overwhelming, but Lost Weekend, which combines all these things, is one of the chillest places to have a cup of coffee on the Lower East Side. Although the vibe is California-tinged, this café is firmly rooted in New York: the excellent beans from Blue Bottle are roasted in Williamsburg and the hot chocolate is from Brooklyn's Mast Brothers. Care is put into each drink as the shop eschews drip coffee in favor of hand-pouring each cup to order. With plenty of seating, Lost Weekend is an ideal place to recharge after a day of visiting local galleries.

OPEN.
Mon-Sun.   8:00am - 8:00pm

OVERVIEW.
Category
Independent
Owner
Chad Eggers and Michael Little
First opened
2011

COFFEE & EQUIPMENT.
Roaster
Blue Bottle Coffee
Machine
La Marzocco FB/80
Grinder
Mazzer Major
Bulk brewer
Pourover is offered in lieu of
drip coffee

PRICES.
Filter / Drip	$3.00
Espresso	$2.75
Cappuccino	$3.50
Latte	$4.00

FOOD.
Baked goods from Baked in Red Hook
and chocolate from Mast Brothers
in Williamsburg.

CONTACT.
(917) 261-2401
www.lostweekendnyc.com
Subway F (Delancey St)

RATING.

COFFEE
4.00 / 5

OVERALL
4.00 / 5

Mudspot

307 East 9th Street, Manhattan, NY 10003 | East Village ....

Mudspot is a downtown New York institution and its burnt orange coffee truck is an Astor Place landmark, frequented by early morning commuters, tourists and students alike. The same orange motif carries over into this permanent café, a cozy spot with a sylvan charm that offers Mud's signature coffee, as well as a full menu of bohemian café fare. The dimly lit interior provides a relaxing environment and if you exit through the back door, you'll feel as though you've stepped into a secret garden. The coffee is strong and flavorful, while the baked goods are prepared fresh in house. Truly embodying the East Village vibe, every aspect of this place is effortlessly cool, right down to the stylish mugs.

FOOD.

A full menu of American café fare including breakfast, lunch and dinner, with fresh housemade baked goods and desserts.

CONTACT.

(212) 228-9074
www.mudnyc.com
mudmail@themudtruck.com
Subway 4,6 (Astor Place)

OPEN.

Mon-Fri.	7:30am - midnight
Sat-Sun.	8:00am - midnight

OVERVIEW.

Category
Multi-independent
Owner
Greg Northrop and Nina Berott
First opened
2000

COFFEE & EQUIPMENT.

Roaster
Mud Coffee
Machine
La Marzocco Linea
Grinder
Mazzer Major Auto
Bulk brewer
Cecilware

PRICES.

Filter / Drip	$2.50
Espresso	$2.50
Cappuccino	$4.50
Latte	$4.50

Other locations
4th Avenue & 8th Street / 22nd Street & Broadway (weekdays) / Union Square West (weekends)

RATING.

COFFEE 3.75 / 5
OVERALL 4.00 / 5 ★★★★☆

The National

8 Rivington Street, Manhattan, NY 10002 | **Lower East Side** ....

OPEN.
Mon-Sun.   8:00am - 4:30pm
(for espresso - the restaurant is
open for dinner)

If you find yourself on the Lower East Side on a rainy day, get thee to The National for an espresso. Decorated with vintage mirrors and an antique motorcycle, this café fits into the trendy local landscape, but displays none of the hectic pretension that plague other places in the area. High-quality Counter Culture coffee is pulled from a top-flight La Marzocco Linea machine and the focus on espresso here (no drip coffees are available) mirrors the relaxed, European-inflected atmosphere. Drink your espresso perched on one of the bar stools or at one of the restaurant's many tables, but just don't pull out your laptop - it'll prevent the other guests from pretending they're in Paris. At night, The National converts into a candle-lit restaurant.

OVERVIEW.
Category
Independent
Owner
Julie Dickstein and Jeremy Hogeland
First opened
2009

COFFEE & EQUIPMENT.
Roaster
Counter Culture
Machine
La Marzocco Linea
Grinder
Mazzer Major

PRICES.
Espresso	$2.50
Cappuccino	$3.50
Latte	$4.00

FOOD.
Full restaurant menu. In the morning, try a popular fried egg sandwich.

CONTACT.
(212) 777-2177
thenationalrestaurantnyc.com
Subway F (2nd Ave)

RATING.

COFFEE
3.75 / 5

OVERALL
3.75 / 5

Ninth Street Espresso

700 East 9th Street, Manhattan, NY 10009 | **East Village** ....

Ninth Street Espresso's Ken Nye is considered one of the founding fathers of the third-wave coffee movement in New York, having established his shop in 2001. Since then, this sleek, minimal shop has set the standard for high-end coffee across the city. With an absurdly affordable drip coffee, a polished, contemporary interior and a relaxing environment, this café is a true coffee destination. The coffee itself is skilfully executed, with espresso that is dark and deeply satisfying, and a truly incredible sweet drip. Ninth Street is as much a coffee purist's dream as it is a cool spot to introduce to visiting friends and holds a significant place in New York coffee history.

OPEN.
Mon-Sun.   7:00am - 8:00pm

OVERVIEW.
Category
Multi-independent
Owner
Ken Nye
First opened
2001

COFFEE & EQUIPMENT.
Roaster
House blend roasted by Dallis
Bros Coffee
Machine
La Marzocco Linea MP
Grinder
Mazzer Robur E
Bulk brewer
AMW Urn Brewer

Other locations
East 10th Street / Chelsea Market

PRICES.

Filter / Drip	$1.50
Espresso	$2.75
Cappuccino	$4.00
Latte	$4.25

FOOD.
A small variety of baked goods
from Balthazar and Downtown
Cookie Company.

CONTACT.
(212) 358-9225
www.ninthstreetespresso.com
info@ninthstreetespresso.com
Subway L (First Ave)

East Village & Lower East Side

RATING.

COFFEE	4.50 / 5
OVERALL	4.50 / 5

Ost Cafe

441 East 12th Street, Manhattan, NY 10009 | **East Village** ································

This Central European-inspired cafe is a versatile spot for coffee seekers where customers can be found both computing and conversing. Visit in the morning to work in the antique dining room or wait until the sun sets, when the computers disappear and the atmosphere becomes more romantic. The interior is spacious and elegant in a quiet kind of way, with a small library of books in the back you can peruse. Ost switches up its espresso between PT's and Intelligentsia's Black Cat depending on the day, with single origins available for cold-brewed iced coffee. The café also hosts wine tastings and jazz performances in the evenings, making this a perfectly lovely date spot.

East Village & Lower East Side

OPEN.

Sun-Thu.	7:30am - 10:00pm
Fri.	7:30am - 11:00pm
Sat.	8:30am - 11:00pm

OVERVIEW.

Category
Independent
Owner
Alex Clark, Aaron Hagedorn,
Kat Maxianova and Lenka Opalena
First opened
2008

COFFEE & EQUIPMENT.

Roaster
Intelligentsia, PT's
and Brooklyn Roasters
Machine
La Marzocco GB/5, 3 groups
Grinder
Mazzer

PRICES.

Filter / Drip	$1.75
Espresso	$2.50
Cappuccino	$4.00
Latte	$4.25

FOOD.

An assortment of baked goods such
as pastries from Ceci Cela Patisserie,
cookies from Westville East down
the street and strudel from Moishe's
over on Second Avenue, as well as
traditional cheese and meat plates
served in the evenings.

CONTACT.

(212) 477-5600
www.ostcafenyc.com
info@ostcafenyc.com
Subway L (First Ave)

RATING.

COFFEE 4.25 / 5	🫘 🫘 🫘 🫘 🫘
OVERALL 4.25 / 5	★ ★ ★ ★ ⯪

42

Prima

58 East 1st Street, Manhattan, NY 10003 | East Village ··································

OPEN.

Mon-Sun. 8:00am - 5:00pm
(for coffee)

Although it transforms into a bar at night, Prima puts on its morning clothes with ease, starting the day as a sleek, uncrowded and light-filled (even on a cloudy day) café. Two long bars lined with stools are a great place for meetings or solitary contemplation over a Ninth Street espresso, which is rich and delicious. In contrast to much of the East Village, Prima doesn't seem concerned with being trendy and is a great place to relax before or after a night on the town.

FOOD.

Pastries from Payard Bakery until 5:00pm, when coffee service ends and a full dinner menu is served.

CONTACT.

(646) 559-4823
www.primanyc.net
Subway F (2nd Ave)

OVERVIEW.

Category
Independent
Owner
Hamid Rashidzada
First opened
2011

COFFEE & EQUIPMENT.

Roaster
Ninth Street Espresso
Machine
La Marzocco FB/80
Grinder
Mazzer Major
Bulk brewer
Fetco

PRICES.

Filter / Drip	$1.50
Espresso	$2.75
Cappuccino	$4.25
Latte	$4.50

RATING.

COFFEE 4.00 / 5	🫘 🫘 🫘 🫘 🫘
OVERALL 3.75 / 5	★ ★ ★ ★ ★

Pushcart Coffee

221 East Broadway, Manhattan, NY 10002 | Lower East Side ....

OPEN.
Mon-Fri.   7:00am - 7:00pm

Pushcart Coffee is a lovely little surprise on the Lower East Side. Outfitted with a hodgepodge of brightly colored chairs and adornments, it's a quirky shop with lots of personality. The atmosphere is relaxed and warm, as are the staff, and the child-friendliness of the shop makes it a perfect spot for a playdate. With Stumptown coffee for moms and dads and Balthazar pastries for the kiddies, Pushcart Coffee is a fun little place with something for everyone.

FOOD.
Pastries, oatmeal and bagels, along with sandwiches and baked goods from Balthazar, Maggie's Kitchen, and gluten-free options from Krumville and Ruby Bakes.

CONTACT.
(212) 876-8065
www.pushcartcoffee.com
info@pushcartcoffee.com
Subway F (East Broadway)

OVERVIEW.
Category
Independent
Owner
Jamie Rogers and Lisa Fischoff
First opened
2011

COFFEE & EQUIPMENT.
Roaster
Stumptown Coffee Roasters
Machine
La Marzocco Linea, 2 groups
Grinder
Mazzer Robur E
Bulk brewer
Fetco

PRICES.
Filter / Drip	$1.75
Espresso	$2.75
Cappuccino	$3.75
Latte	$3.75

RATING.

COFFEE
3.75 / 5

OVERALL
3.75 / 5

The Randolph at Broome

349 Broome Street, Manhattan, NY 10013 | **Lower East Side** ....

OPEN.
Mon-Sun.   7:00am - 5:00pm
(for coffee)

Going to a bar during daylight might seem a depressing idea, but popular nightspot The Randolph is one of the coziest places for a cup of coffee on the Lower East Side. While French press is available, the emphasis is on giving coffee the cocktail treatment - minus the booze. This translates into a menu of sweet, frothy, coffee-based drinks made with fine ingredients and unique flavor combinations, all available hot or iced. You can order your drink to go, but these coffees are designed to be sipped at the bar, as many involve a theatrical presentation. Coffee snobs may scoff at the lack of espresso here, but they certainly won't at the extensive list of roasters that supply the beans. If you're interested in mixing business with pleasure, peruse the extensive list of coffee-infused cocktails, or wait until 5pm, when the The Randolph turns back into a classic New York bar.

FOOD.
Muffins from Blue Sky Bakery.

OVERVIEW.
Category
Independent
Owner
Hari Nathan Kalyan
First opened
2010

COFFEE & EQUIPMENT.
Roaster
Oslo, Roasting Plant, Counter Culture, Dark Matter and Intelligentsia
Grinder
Bunn

PRICES.
Filter / Drip $2.50

CONTACT.
(212) 274-0667
randolphnyc.com
info@randolphnyc.com
Subway J (Bowery)

RATING.

| COFFEE 4.00 / 5 | |
| OVERALL 4.00 / 5 |  |

Starbucks Astor Place

13-25 Astor Place, Manhattan, NY 10003 | **East Village** ....

OPEN.

Mon-Fri.	5:30am - 1:00am
Sat.	6:00am - 1:00am
Sun.	6:00am - midnight

The largest of all the Starbucks stores in New York, this East Village spot is constantly packed with visiting tourists, neighborhood regulars and college students seeking a caffeine boost. It's spacious for sure, with lots of tables at which to perch, work and meet, although it's just as popular for a grab and go at any time. The store serves as a serene stop for anyone bustling through this busy part of town - the atrium-like space with its wraparound windows makes this one of the most picturesque Starbucks stores around and the trusty menu means that even in crazy New York, you can still get whatever drink makes you feel at home.

FOOD.

A menu of baked goods, sandwiches, salads, pre-made plates and other small snacks.

CONTACT.

(212) 982-3753
www.starbucks.com
Subway 6 (Astor Place), N,R (8th St - NYU)

OVERVIEW.

Category
Chain
Owner
Starbucks Coffee Company
First opened
1995

COFFEE & EQUIPMENT.

Roaster
Starbucks
Machine
Starbucks Mastrena
Grinder
Starbucks Mastrena and Ditting
Bulk brewer
Bunn

PRICES.

Filter / Drip	$1.85
Espresso	$1.95
Cappuccino	$3.25
Latte	$3.25

Other locations
Many locations throughout the city

RATING.

COFFEE	3.75 / 5
OVERALL	3.75 / 5

Greenwich Village & Neighboring

Fashionable, fun and creative, the neighbourhoods of Greenwich Village, Soho, Noho and Chelsea are all popular for their vibrant cultural activity. Greenwich Village, once the home of the Beat Generation, still maintains its bohemian and creative energy, but is now also home to an array of restaurants, shops and theatres. Soho and Noho are diverse shopping meccas, while Chelsea has some of the best art galleries in the city, as well as the new Highline, a park built on a defunct elevated subway line.

Blue Bottle Coffee Chelsea

450 West 15th Street, Manhattan, NY 10011 | **Chelsea** ....

Blue Bottle's new Chelsea location is a must for any coffee enthusiast visiting New York. Featuring the same familiar set-up downstairs as at the Brooklyn store - a full drip bar, cold-brewed offerings, gourmet bakery items and a full menu of espresso drinks - it's what can be found upstairs that makes this place unique: a six-seat bar, where coffee is a culinary experience rather than a quick shot-and-go. Guests are greeted with cloth napkins, palate-cleansing cascara tea (made from the skin of coffee cherries) and a varied menu of single-origin coffees brewed using the siphon or Nel drip styles.

This ceremony is as fun as it is delicious and the entire experience constitutes coffee with style, served by skilled and knowledgeable baristas.

OPEN.

Mon-Fri.	7:00am - 7:00pm
Sat-Sun.	9:00am - 7:00pm

OVERVIEW.

Category
Chain
Owner
James Freeman
First opened
February 2012

COFFEE & EQUIPMENT.

Roaster
Blue Bottle Coffee
Machine
La Marzocco Strada MP
Grinder
Mazzer

Other locations
Williamsburg / Rockefeller Center / Highline (summer only)

PRICES.

Filter / Drip	$2.75
Espresso	$2.75
Cappuccino	$3.50
Latte	$4.00

FOOD.

A small assortment of treats, both savory and sweet, all lovingly prepared in house and with organic and locally produced ingredients.

Siphon or Nel drip coffees and **brioche toast** are offered upstairs in the siphon bar 11:00am - 5:00pm

CONTACT.

www.bluebottlecoffee.net
info@bluebottlecoffee.net
Subway A, C, E, L (14th St - 8th Ave)

RATING.

COFFEE
4.50 / 5

OVERALL
4.50 / 5
★★★★⯪

Café Grumpy Chelsea

224 West 20th Street, Manhattan, NY 10011 | **Chelsea** ....

Nestled on a charming, tree-lined street, this Chelsea location is the coziest of all the Café Grumpy shops. Patrons are greeted at a low counter and invited to watch their lattes and individually brewed cups being prepared by friendly and helpful baristas. The homey atmosphere extends to Grumpy's no-computer policy, which asks that technology be put away in lieu of a friendlier experience - single-origin coffees and homemade goodies definitely taste better when shared with friends.

OPEN.

Mon-Fri.	7:00am - 8:00pm
Sat.	7:30am - 8:00pm
Sun.	7:30am - 7:30pm

OVERVIEW.

Category
Multi-independent
Owner
Chris Timbrell and Caroline Bell
First opened
2006

COFFEE & EQUIPMENT.

Roaster
Café Grumpy
Machine
Synesso Hydra, 3 groups
Grinder
Mazzer Robur E x 2, Mazzer Super Jolly, Ditting
Bulk brewer
Clover x 2

Other locations
Park Slope / Lower East Side / Greenpoint

PRICES.

Filter / Drip	$2.75
Espresso	$2.75
Cappuccino	$3.75
Latte	$4.00

FOOD.

An array of freshly baked goods made at the Café Grumpy bakery on Essex Street in Manhattan.

CONTACT.

(212) 255-5511
www.cafegrumpy.com
cafegrumpy@gmail.com
Subway 1 (18th St) and A, C, E, L (14th St - 8th Ave)

RATING.

COFFEE	
4.50 / 5	🫘🫘🫘🫘🫘
OVERALL	
4.50 / 5	★★★★⯨

Gasoline Alley Coffee

TOP 30

331 Lafayette Street, Manhattan, NY 10012 | **Noho**

OPEN.

Mon-Fri.	7:00am - 7:00pm
Sat.	8:00am - 7:00pm
Sun.	9:00am - 7:00pm

Gasoline Alley takes its name from the area's status as a car repair district during the 1960s, and although the industrial-chic atmosphere remains, this area now provides a different kind of tune-up. Located in the wedge-shaped block where Lafayette Street and Broadway converge, entrances on each side of this café (and open windows in the summer) give the petite shop an open, airy feel. Baristas here are careful and serious, and the Intelligentsia espresso is dark and full-bodied. Cold kombucha is available on tap in rotating flavors - all are great palate-cleansers but mint-apple is particularly refreshing.

FOOD.

Pastries from Ceci Cela, chocolate from Mast Brothers. Kombucha on tap is also offered.

CONTACT.

www.gasolinealleycoffee.com
info@gasolinealleycoffee.com
Subway 6 (Bleecker St)

OVERVIEW.

Category
Independent
Owner
Nicolas Carnevale and Neville Ross
First opened
2011

COFFEE & EQUIPMENT.

Roaster
Intelligentsia Coffee
Machine
La Marzocco GB/5
Grinder
Mahlkönig
Bulk brewer
Fetco

PRICES.

Filter / Drip	$2.00
Espresso	$2.75
Cappuccino	$4.00
Latte	$4.25

RATING.

COFFEE 4.50 / 5

OVERALL 4.25 / 5

53

The Grey Dog

90 University Place, Manhattan, NY 10003 | Greenwich Village ....

OPEN.

Mon-Fri.	6:30am - 11:30pm
Sat-Sun.	7:00am - 11:30pm

This cozy spot on University Place is as popular for brunch as it is for an evening date, with beer on tap and a house espresso roast. The kitschy down-home atmosphere is quirky and enchanting: twinkle-lights adorn the walls and tables decorated using the maps of different states will make any customer feel at home. The coffee is consistently good and a mug of the drip is bottomless if you stay to drink it. Pair this with a sizeable sandwich or salad and you'll be one happy camper.

FOOD.

A menu of all-American café fare with breakfast specialties, salads, sandwiches, soups and an array of baked goods all prepared in house.

CONTACT.

(212) 414-4739
thegreydog.com
thegreydog@yahoo.com
Subway N, R, W, 4, 5, 6, L (Union Sq / 14th St)

Other locations
Mulberry Street / West 16th Street

OVERVIEW.

Category
Multi-independent
Owner
Peter Adrian and David Ethan
First opened
1996

COFFEE & EQUIPMENT.

Roaster
The Grey Dog
Machine
Magister, 2 groups
Grinder
Bunn
Bulk brewer
Grindmaster

PRICES.

Filter / Drip	$2.07
Espresso	$2.50
Cappuccino	$4.12
Latte	$4.12

RATING.

COFFEE 3.50 / 5	🫘 🫘 🫘 🫘 🫘
OVERALL 3.75 / 5	★ ★ ★ ★ ★

Ground Support

399 West Broadway, Manhattan, NY 10012 | **Soho** ....

Picnic-tabled Soho mainstay Ground Support is a necessity in this shopping mecca of a neighborhood. It's always busy in the morning, dispensing Intelligentsia Black Cat espresso and shelling out fresh, locally sourced muffins and bagels, but as busy as it gets, it never feels frenzied here. The shop itself is beautifully understated: a bright, elegantly simple space fitted out in natural wood. Skilled baristas pull beautifully balanced lattes and brew refreshing iced coffees, and it almost feels like perpetual summer at this happy spot in the middle of the buzzing city.

Greenwich Village & Neighboring

OPEN.

Mon-Fri.	7:00am - 8:00pm
Sat-Sun.	8:00am - 8:00pm

OVERVIEW.

Category
Independent
Owner
Steven Sadoff
First opened
2009

COFFEE & EQUIPMENT.

Roaster
Intelligentsia Coffee
Machine
La Marzocco Linea, 3 groups
Grinder
Mazzer Robur E
Bulk brewer
Fetco

PRICES.

Filter / Drip	$1.50
Espresso	$2.50
Cappuccino	$3.50
Latte	$3.50

FOOD.

Baked goods from local bakeries and fresh, housemade sandwiches and salads throughout the day.

CONTACT.

(212) 219-8722
www.groundsupportcafe.com
grndspprt@gmail.com
Subway C, E (Spring St) or 6 (Spring St)

RATING.

COFFEE
4.50 / 5

OVERALL
4.50 / 5
★★★★½

Housing Works Bookstore Cafe

126 Crosby Street, Manhattan, NY 10012 | **Soho** ....

OPEN.

Mon-Fri.	10:00am - 9:00pm
Sat-Sun.	10:00am - 5:00pm

A lovely café with a wonderful ethos, this bookstore and coffee shop is a part of the Housing Works organization, a not-for-profit that works to combat both homelessness and HIV AIDS with advocacy, services and sustainable business. All proceeds from the bookstore and café go towards the mission and everyone who works here is a volunteer. The café is warm and comfortable with lots of seating and the coffee is well made with Intelligentsia beans. Baked goods come from local shops, while all the salads, sandwiches and other heartier items are prepared fresh in store. The café also hosts events such as The Moth, another not-for-profit that organizes live storytelling evenings.

FOOD.

Baked goods from neighborhood suppliers such as Balthazar, and salads, sandwiches and the like all prepared in house.

CONTACT.

(212) 334-3324
www.housingworks.org
Subway B, D, F, M (Broadway - Lafayette St) or 4, 6 (Bleecker St)

OVERVIEW.

Category
Independent
Owner
Housing Works
First opened
1990

COFFEE & EQUIPMENT.

Roaster
Intelligentsia Coffee
Machine
La Marzocco Linea, 2 groups
Grinder
La Marzocco Swift
Bulk brewer
Fetco

PRICES.

Filter / Drip	$1.50
Espresso	$2.50
Cappuccino	$3.50
Latte	$3.50

RATING.

COFFEE	
3.75 / 5	🫘🫘🫘🫘🫘
OVERALL	
3.75 / 5	★★★★☆

McNally Jackson Café

52 Prince Street, Manhattan, NY 10012 | **Soho** ....

OPEN.

Mon-Sat.	10:00am - 10:00pm
Sun.	10:00am - 9:00pm

McNally Jackson is a wonderful independent Soho bookshop that remains one of the best in the city. It also happens to be home to an adorable café, and constitutes the perfect marriage of coffee and culture. Stumptown coffee is meticulously served to accompany that book you noticed while browsing, and the space is bright and cozy. Some books are suspended from the ceiling, while others have been converted into mug coasters, and the literary motif is as fitting as it is charming. McNally Jackson is so infectiously well-versed, you may feel compelled to start waxing lyrical yourself.

FOOD.

Assorted housemade sandwiches, seasonal soups and salads, and baked goods from neighborhood bakeries such as Balthazar and Pickle Petunia.

CONTACT.

(212) 274-1160
www.mcnallyjackson.com
info@mcnallyjackson.com
Subway 4, 6 (Spring St) or N, R (Prince St) or B, D, F, M (Broadway - Lafayette St)

OVERVIEW.

Category
Independent
Owner
Sarah McNally
First opened
2004

COFFEE & EQUIPMENT.

Roaster
Stumptown Coffee Roasters
Machine
La Marzocco Linea
Grinder
Mazzer Luigi
Bulk brewer
Fetco

PRICES.

Filter / Drip	$1.99
Espresso	$1.99
Cappuccino	$3.25
Latte	$3.25

RATING.

COFFEE 3.75 / 5	🫘 🫘 🫘 🫘 🫘
OVERALL 3.75 / 5	★ ★ ★ ✬ ☆

Porto Rico Importing Company

201 Bleecker Street, Manhattan, NY 10012 | Greenwich Village ....

OPEN.

Mon-Fri.	8:00am - 9:00pm
Sat.	9:00am - 9:00pm
Sun.	12:00pm - 7:00pm

This New York coffee wholesaler and coffee bar isn't interested in following trends, as it is one of New York's best-established coffee institutions. This is a family business, passed down to current owner Peter Longo who runs the small group of stores with an active hand. Where possible, he works directly with farmers in countries such as Colombia, El Salvador and Jamaica, but roasts his beans locally in Williamsburg to fit profiles that range from single origin to flavored roast. An extensive collection of coffee and tea equipment is also available.

FOOD.

An assortment of pastries from Settepani Bakery in Williamsburg.

CONTACT.

(212) 477-5421
www.portorico.com
questions@portorico.com
Subway 1, 2 (Houston St) or A, C, E (Spring St)

Other locations
St. Marks / Grand Street / Essex Street

OVERVIEW.

Category
Multi-independent
Owner
Peter Longo
First opened
1907

COFFEE & EQUIPMENT.

Roaster
Porto Rico
Machine
Astoria
Grinder
Astoria, Ditting
Bulk brewer
Fetco

PRICES.

Filter / Drip	$1.25
Espresso	$1.35
Cappuccino	$2.75
Latte	$2.75

RATING.

COFFEE	
4.00 / 5	🌰🌰🌰🌰🌰
OVERALL	
3.75 / 5	★★★★★

PORTS Coffee & Tea Company

251 West 23rd Street, Manhattan, NY 10011 | Chelsea ....

OPEN.

Mon-Fri.	7:00am - 8:00pm
Sat-Sun.	8:00am - 6:00pm

OVERVIEW.

Category
Independent
Owner
Nina and Larry Adams
First opened
2011

PORTS is something of an anomaly: although tiny and on a very busy street, it's definitely a neighborhood spot, thanks in part to some of the friendliest baristas in town, who put meticulous care into each cup. The PORTS espresso rotates between Stumptown and the LA-based Handsome Coffee Roasters, or ask your barista to recommend something from the single-origin pourover or fine organic tea menu. Nautical rope and antique maps decorate the space, making this an ideal place to dock between journeys.

COFFEE & EQUIPMENT.

Roaster
Stumptown Coffee Roasters, Handsome Coffee Roasters
Machine
La Marzocco GB/5
Grinder
Mazzer

FOOD.

Cookies from Scratch Bakery, chocolate bars from Mast Brothers, pastries by Ovenly and cookies by Downtown Cookie Company.

PRICES.

Filter / Drip	$2.00
Espresso	$2.75
Cappuccino	$3.75
Latte	$4.25

CONTACT.

(646) 290-6151
www.portsnyc.com
info@portsnyc.com
Subway 1 (23rd St), C, E (23rd St)

Features a constantly rotating menu of **single-origin coffees** made with Hario kettles and Beehouse drippers

RATING.

COFFEE
4.25 / 5

OVERALL
4.00 / 5

Saturdays Surf NYC

31 Crosby Street, Manhattan, NY 10013 | Soho ·······································

OPEN.

Mon-Fri.	8:30am - 6:30pm
Sat-Sun.	10:00am - 6:30pm

An alternative coffee bar for the fashionable set, this popular Soho shop is primarily a surf store with boards, gear and correspondingly grunge-chic clothes for those trips to the beach. But as well as hanging ten, you can also take five at the mean espresso bar where La Colombe coffee is served. There's nothing in the way of seating inside the store, but once spring rolls around, a spacious patio opens out the back, with plenty of seats and tables at which to soak up some city sun and dream of the perfect break.

PRICES.

Filter / Drip	$2.00
Espresso	$2.50
Cappuccino	$3.50
Latte	$4.00

CONTACT.

(212) 966-7875
www.saturdaysnyc.com
store@saturdaysnyc.com
Subway 4, 6 (Canal St)

OVERVIEW.

Category
Independent
Owner
Morgan Collett, Josh Rosen
and Colin Tunstall
First opened
2009

COFFEE & EQUIPMENT.

Roaster
La Colombe Torrefaction
Machine
La Marzocco Linea, 3 groups
Grinder
Mazzer Luigi
Bulk brewer
Bunn

RATING.

COFFEE 4.00 / 5	🫘 🫘 🫘 🫘 🫘
OVERALL 3.75 / 5	★ ★ ★ ★ ★

The Smile

26 Bond Street, Manhattan, NY 10012 | **Noho** ....

OPEN.

Mon-Fri.	8:00am - midnight
Sat-Sun.	10:00am - midnight

A beautiful dark wooden restaurant with a rustic feel, this place is a serious eatery that also offers serious coffee. Amazing food is accompanied by well-balanced lattes and fresh French press coffee. The restaurant gets packed with Soho-bound shoppers and families come brunch time, but is nice and quiet during weekday lunch hours. The space has an aged elegance that recalls a rural general store, but the effortlessly cool downstairs shop brings a sophisticated downtown Manhattan edge. This a great place to meet and mingle for a bite and a coffee, both of which are equally good.

FOOD.

A menu of New American fare, with brunch on the weekends and a full service of items throughout the day.

CONTACT.

(646) 329-5836
thesmilenyc.com
Subway B, D, F, M (Broadway - Lafayette St) or 4, 6 (Bleecker St)

OVERVIEW.

Category
Independent
Owner
Carlos Quirarte and Matt Kliegman
First opened
2009

COFFEE & EQUIPMENT.

Roaster
Plowshares
Machine
Faema E61
Grinder
Santos

PRICES.

Filter / Drip	$3.00
Espresso	$2.50
Cappuccino	$3.50
Latte	$3.75

RATING.

COFFEE	
3.75 / 5	🫘🫘🫘🫘🫘
OVERALL	
4.25 / 5	★★★★✩

Think Coffee

248 Mercer Street, Manhattan, NY 10012 | **Greenwich Village** ....

OPEN.

Mon-Fri.	7:00am - 11:00pm
Sat-Sun.	8:00am - midnight

OVERVIEW.

Category
Multi-independent
Owner
Jason Scherr
First opened
2005

COFFEE & EQUIPMENT.

Roaster
Porto Rico
Machine
La Marzocco
Grinder
Bunn
Bulk brewer
Fetco

PRICES.

Filter / Drip	$1.85
Espresso	$2.05
Cappuccino	$3.48
Latte	$3.48

Other locations
Bleecker Street / NYU Bookstore /
4th Avenue near Union Square /
8th Avenue

This vast but cozy branch of the Think Coffee mini-chain serves as an unofficial NYU campus and, as a result, the space has a youthful buzzing energy unlike any other shop in town, aided by a constant stream of thumping music. While not really a place to relax, this is the perfect spot to work for hours on end, meet a new friend, or maybe take a weekend date. Staff are friendly and attentive despite the eternally long line and serve a reliable menu of coffees, as well as a sizeable selection of teas, juices and lunch items. The espresso is strong, and is delicious either on its own or in a well-balanced latte.

FOOD.

A breakfast menu including bagels and oatmeal, as well as sandwiches, salads and a wide array of baked goods from local purveyors.

CONTACT.

thinkcoffeenyc.com
thinkcoffee@msn.com
Subway N, R (8th St - NYU) or B, D, F, M (Broadway - Lafayette St)

RATING.

COFFEE 4.00 / 5

OVERALL 4.00 / 5

Third Rail Coffee

240 Sullivan Street, Manhattan, NY 10012 | Greenwich Village

OPEN.

Mon-Fri.	7:00am - 8:00pm
Sat-Sun.	8:00am - 8:00pm

Tables are sparse and tightly packed at this tiny Greenwich Village café, so it would behoove you to plan your coffee to-go. Third Rail drip coffee is appropriately strong and a perfect way to jump-start your day, while pastries come from New York staples such as Ceci Cela and Balthazar. Coffee and pastry in hand, stroll over to nearby Washington Square Park to take in some music or people watching. If you're lucky, you might see celebrity chef Mario Batali stroll by amid a mix of NYU students, New York locals and tourists.

FOOD.
A selection of baked goods from Ceci Cela Patisserie and Balthazar.

CONTACT.
www.thirdrailcoffee.com
info@thirdrailcoffee.com
Subway A, C, E, B, D, F, M (W. 4th St)

OVERVIEW.
Category
Independent
Owner
Humberto Ricardo and Rita McCaffrey
First opened
2009

COFFEE & EQUIPMENT.
Roaster
Intelligentsia Coffee, Stumptown Coffee Roasters
Machine
La Marzocco GB/5
Grinder
Mazzer Robur E
Bulk brewer
Fetco

PRICES.
Filter / Drip	$1.85
Espresso	$2.75
Cappuccino	$3.75
Latte	$3.75

RATING.

COFFEE 4.50 / 5

OVERALL 4.50 / 5 ★★★★⯪

Greenwich Village & Neighboring

Midtown & Gramercy

Midtown is fast-paced, bustling and one of the greatest commercial centers in the world. The Empire State Building, The New York Public Library, MoMA and the core of New York's theatre district – including the bright lights of Times Square - can all be found in Midtown. This area is also home to the small and elegant Gramercy, a quiet neighbourhood with the private, preserved Gramercy Park at its center: a lovely reminder of New York's Victorian history.

Birch Coffee

5 East 27th Street, Manhattan, NY 10016 | **Midtown East** ···

Tucked away inside the playfully elegant Gershwin Hotel, Birch is a charming retreat from midtown Manhattan. Its secluded library upstairs is a strong contender for the coziest room in the borough and is the perfect place to read or study on a rainy day. Grab a delicious housemade treat and browse the used books, then as the sun sets, order a glass of wine or a beer and partake in the menu of salads and sandwiches. The space is relaxed and welcoming, as are the baristas, and owners Jeremy and Paul can often be spotted greeting regulars and pulling shots behind the counter. The coffee itself consistently hits the spot: the Birch Blend is dark and deeply satisfying and the espresso has a clean, almost sweet taste.

OPEN.

Mon-Fri.	7:00am - 9:00pm
Sat.	8:00am - 9:00pm
Sun.	8:00am - 8:00pm

OVERVIEW.

Category
Independent
Owner
Jeremy Lyman and Paul Schlader
First opened
2009

COFFEE & EQUIPMENT.

Roaster
Birch Coffee
Machine
La Marzocco Strada MP
Grinder
Mazzer, Bunn
Bulk brewer
Fetco

PRICES.

Filter / Drip	$2.50
Espresso	$2.75 (triple ristretto)
Cappuccino	$3.50
Latte	$3.50

FOOD.

A locally sourced menu of breakfast options, sandwiches and salads served throughout the day, with housemade cookies, muffins, brownies and other baked goods.

CONTACT.

(212) 686-1444
www.birchcoffee.com
jeremy@birchcoffee.com
Subway N, R (28th St) or 4,6 (28th St)

RATING.

COFFEE 4.25 / 5	🫘 🫘 🫘 🫘 🫘
OVERALL 4.25 / 5	★ ★ ★ ★ ⯪

Caffebene

1661 Broadway, Manhattan, NY 10019 | **Midtown West** ....

The first American outpost of this South Korean chain, Caffebene combines specialty coffee shop and international conglomerate to create something new. Traditional espresso drinks are offered alongside specialties such as the Misugaru latte, a sweet drink made from rice, barley and other multigrains. But look closer to find espresso made on twin La Marzocco GB/5 espresso machines, fresh pastries from local bakeries and coffee roasted by Chicago's Metropolis Coffee Company and it becomes apparent that Caffebene is artisanal coffee on a global level, a chain that pays respect to local cultures but brings its own flavor. Caffebene is a remarkably good, wonderfully unexpected find in hectic Times Square.

OPEN.
Mon-Sun.   5:30am - 2:00am

OVERVIEW.
Category
Chain
Owner
Sun-Kwon Kim
First opened
2012

COFFEE & EQUIPMENT.
Roaster
Metropolis Coffee Company
Machine
La Marzocco GB/5, 3 groups
Grinder
Mazzer Robur E
Bulk brewer
Fetco

PRICES.
Filter / Drip	$1.75
Espresso	$2.25
Cappuccino	$3.25
Latte	$3.15

FOOD.
A vast menu of breakfast options, fresh waffles, smoothies, sandwiches, salads, gelato and pastries from such local favorites as Dough and Blue Sky Bakery.

CONTACT.
(212) 586-2010
www.thecaffebene.com
info@caffebene.com
Subway 1 (50th St) or C, E (50th St) or N, Q, R (49th St)

RATING.

COFFEE	
4.00 / 5	🫘 🫘 🫘 🫘 🫘

OVERALL	
4.25 / 5	★ ★ ★ ★ ★

Culture Espresso Bar

72 West 38th Street, Manhattan, NY 10018 | **Midtown East** ....

This busy café is a wonderful respite from the Times Square rush, an excellent coffee shop that substitutes the hustle and bustle of the nearby theater district for more comforting stimulants. Anything ordered from these attentive and careful baristas is excellent and that goes for the food choices too. The house-prepared sandwiches are fresh and satisfying, and the gourmet baked goods, delivered fresh from Scratchbread, are inventive and mind-bogglingly delicious. So take a break, enjoy a beautifully prepared cup of coffee and watch the Midtown rat race go by.

OPEN.

Mon-Fri.	7:00am - 7:00pm
Sat-Sun.	8:00am - 7:00pm

OVERVIEW.

Category
Independent
Owner
Jody LoCascio
First opened
2009

COFFEE & EQUIPMENT.

Roaster
Changes depending on the season.
Familiar roasters are Stumptown, PTs,
Intelligentsia Coffee and Toby's Estate
Machine
La Marzocco Strada MP, 3 groups
Grinder
Mazzer doserless Robur E,
Anfim, Ditting
Bulk brewer
Fetco

PRICES.

Filter / Drip	$2.00
Espresso	$2.50
Cappuccino	$3.75
Latte	$4.00

FOOD.

Baked goods delivered fresh from
Dough and Blue Sky Bakery
in Brooklyn.

CONTACT.

(212) 302-0200
www.cultureespresso.com
culture@cultureespresso.com
Subway B, D, F, M (42nd St - Bryant Pk)

RATING.

COFFEE	
4.50 / 5	🫘 🫘 🫘 🫘 🫘

OVERALL	
4.50 / 5	★ ★ ★ ★ ⯪

Irving Farm Coffee Company

71 Irving Place, Manhattan, NY 10003 | **Gramercy** ....

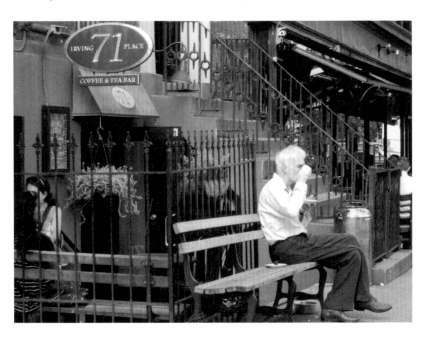

This Gramercy area café hails from the Hudson Valley, where its roastery stands on a renovated farm. Hanging out at this cozy shop, settled in the bottom of a charming brownstone on quiet Irving Place, you'll feel like you could be in upstate New York yourself. The atmosphere is comfortable and homey, and although it's a little snug in terms of seating, a table is never really hard to come by. The coffee is consistently good and Irving Farm sources its baked goods from some of the best local purveyors in the city. This straightforward café doesn't take itself too seriously and is a popular neighborhood spot.

OPEN.

Mon-Wed.	7:00am - 10:00pm
Thu-Fri.	7:00am - 11:00pm
Sat.	8:00am - 11:00pm
Sun.	8:00am - 10:00pm

OVERVIEW.

Category
Multi-independent
Owner
Steven Leven and David Elwell
First opened
1996

COFFEE & EQUIPMENT.

Roaster
Irving Farm Coffee
Machine
La Marzocco Linea, 2 groups
Grinder
Mazzer, Bunn
Bulk brewer
Fetco

Other locations
7th Avenue / W. 79th Street

PRICES.

Filter / Drip	$1.95
Espresso	$2.50
Cappuccino	$3.50
Latte	$4.25

FOOD.

Fresh salads and sandwiches, and croissants from Balthazar.

CONTACT.

(212) 475-5200
www.irvingfarm.com
customerservice@irvingfarm.com
Subway N, R, W, 4, 5, 6, L
(Union Sq / 14th St)

RATING.

COFFEE
3.50 / 5

OVERALL
4.00 / 5

Knave

118 West 57th Street, Manhattan, NY 10019 | **Midtown West** ....

OPEN.

Mon-Sun.　　8:00am - midnight

Nestled in a corridor of the Le Parker Meridien Hotel in midtown Manhattan, Knave is a coffee bar with a mischievous spirit. The décor here is charmingly opulent - rich red drapes, abundant tassles and votive candles fit perfectly with the dark and sinfully divine coffee on offer from the skilled baristas. Primarily a bar that doubles as an entrance to the hotel, Knave might not be a place to sit for hours perusing your copy of Dante's Inferno, but it is a wonderful spot for a soul to wait in limbo for a while.

FOOD.

A menu of European-inspired bites such as pastries in the morning and small plates in the evenings.

CONTACT.

(212) 708-7392

www.parkermeridien.com

Subway N, Q, R (57th St - 7th Ave) or F (57th St)

OVERVIEW.

Category
Independent
Owner
Le Parker Meridien
First opened
2009

COFFEE & EQUIPMENT.

Roaster
Counter Culture
Machine
La Marzocco FB/80
Grinder
Mazzer

PRICES.

Espresso	$4.00
Cappuccino	$6.00
Latte	$6.00

RATING.

COFFEE	
4.25 / 5	🫘🫘🫘🫘🫘
OVERALL	
4.25 / 5	★★★★⯪

Lucid Café

311 Lexington Avenue, Manhattan, NY 10016 | Midtown East

OPEN.

Mon-Fri.	7:00am - 6:00pm
Sat.	8:00am - 6:00pm
Sun.	8:00am - 3:00pm

A collage of postcards from international tourists who've visited Lucid Café greets customers at the entrance and it's easy to see why this venue is so beloved. Tiny and intimate, this is a family-owned neighborhood shop. A café this cozy in Midtown is rare enough, but Lucid takes its coffee to the next level with its attention to detail. The rich Counter Culture espresso is expertly pulled from a top-of-the-line machine and the drip, from a Japanese slow-dripper, is refreshingly complex. If you're in the mood for something sweet and less caffeinated, the green tea latte never disappoints.

FOOD.

A small selection of housemade cookies and other pastries.

CONTACT.

(212) 867-3490
lucidcafe@naver.com
Subway 4, 5, 6 (Grand Central)

OVERVIEW.

Category
Independent
Owner
Namhee Han and Hojin Han
First opened
2010

COFFEE & EQUIPMENT.

Roaster
Counter Culture
Machine
La Marzocco FB/80
Grinder
Mazzer Robur
Bulk brewer
Fetco

PRICES.

Filter / Drip	$2.25
Espresso	$2.75
Cappuccino	$4.00
Latte	$4.25

RATING.

COFFEE 4.00 / 5	
OVERALL 4.00 / 5	

Midtown & Gramercy

Maialino

2 Lexington Avenue, Manhattan, NY 10010 | **Gramercy** ....

OPEN.

Mon-Thu.	7:30am - 10:30pm
Fri.	7:30am - 11:00pm
Sat-Sun.	10:00am - 11:00pm

Coffee is an afterthought at many fine restaurants, but this is not the case at Maialino, a beautiful, award-winning eatery inside the Gramercy Park Hotel. Here coffee is prepared with as much care and expertise as the food, which is considered among the best Italian fare in the city. Breakfast customers can order a seasonal single origin from the pourover bar, or accompany lunch or dinner with a Counter Culture espresso. Although the restaurant itself warrants a substantial visit, casual patrons can still sit at the bar, look out over Gramercy Park and enjoy a coffee without feeling out of place.

FOOD.

Maialino is a Roman trattoria with an Italian menu including housemade pastries, egg dishes and panini sandwiches for breakfast, with a full menu of pastas, entrees and the like continued into the day.

CONTACT.

(212) 777-2410
www.maialinonyc.com
info@maialinonyc.com
Subway 4, 6 (23rd St)

OVERVIEW.

Category
Independent
Owner
Danny Meyer's Union Square Hospitality Group
First opened
2009

COFFEE & EQUIPMENT.

Roaster
Counter Culture
Machine
La Marzocco FB/80, 3 groups
Grinder
Mazzer Major and Mazzer Robur
Bulk brewer
Fetco

PRICES.

Filter / Drip	$3.50
Espresso	$3.25
Cappuccino	$4.50
Latte	$4.75

RATING.

COFFEE 4.25 / 5	🫘 🫘 🫘 🫘 🫘
OVERALL 4.25 / 5	★ ★ ★ ★ ☆

Starbucks Times Square

1585 Broadway, Manhattan, NY 10036 | **Midtown West** ....

OPEN.

Mon-Thu.	6:00am - 1:00am
Fri-Sat.	6:00am - 2:00am
Sun.	6:00am - 1:00am

OVERVIEW.

Category
Chain
Owner
Starbucks Coffee Company
First opened
2011

COFFEE & EQUIPMENT.

Roaster
Starbucks
Machine
Starbucks Mastrena
Grinder
Starbucks Mastrena and Ditting
Bulk brewer
Bunn

FOOD.

A menu of baked goods, sandwiches, salads and other small snacks.

CONTACT.

(212) 541-7515
www.starbucks.com
Subway 1 (50th St) or C, E (50th St) or N, Q, R (49th St)

Taking a cue from its star-studded surroundings, this flagship Starbucks store puts the customer at centre-stage. The front of the store is a technological hub, with large screens for social media, a photo booth and an interactive map of Times Square. Out back has a traditional Starbucks feel, with the same dependable menu of drinks and snacks, and a small area for seating. Venture around the bend and find the Starbucks Reserve Bar, a brew bar featuring Starbucks single origin and specialty coffee blends, all brewed to order on a Clover machine. This is Starbucks at its grandest - a fascinating marriage of glitz and comfort, ceremony and familiarity - and while you're waiting for your latte to arrive, take a look up: you'll find the spotlight is trained on you.

PRICES.

Filter / Drip	$1.85
Espresso	$1.95
Cappuccino	$3.25
Latte	$3.25

Other locations
Many locations throughout the city

RATING.

COFFEE 4.00 / 5	🫘 🫘 🫘 🫘 🫘
OVERALL 4.00 / 5	★ ★ ★ ★ ★

Stumptown Coffee Roasters

18 West 29th Street, Manhattan, NY 10001 | **Midtown West** ....

Stumptown now supplies dozens of shops and restaurants across the city, but this shop was New York's first introduction to the Portland-born roaster. A small and bustling bar situated in the front of the trendy Ace Hotel, this outpost has become a mecca for coffee lovers across the boroughs. If you're in a rush, throw your espresso back at the tiny bar and look out over 29th Street, or take your cup into the Ace's stylish lobby - a cavernous, mood-lit space decorated with antiques and populated by young jet-setters and hip midtown businessmen. Being as popular as it is, the space is often crowded, but there's lots of seating and you'll feel like Eloise's older, cooler sibling while you sip what is widely regarded as some of the best coffee in the city, if not the country.

OPEN.

Mon-Fri.	6:00am - 8:00pm
Sat-Sun.	7:00am - 8:00pm

OVERVIEW.

Category
Chain
Owner
Duane Sorenson and
TSG Consumer Partners
First opened
2009

COFFEE & EQUIPMENT.

Roaster
Stumptown Coffee Roasters
Machine
La Marzocco Mistral, 3 groups
Grinder
Mazzer doserless

Other locations
Portland / Seattle

PRICES.

Filter / Drip	$2.25
Espresso	$3.00
Cappuccino	$3.75
Latte	$3.75

FOOD.

A small selection of baked goods from
Momofuku Milk Bar, Ovenly, Ceci Cela,
Doughnut Plant and Jezalin's.

CONTACT.

(212) 679-2222
www.stumptowncoffee.com
info@stumptowncoffee.com
Subway N, R (28th St) or 4, 6 (28th St)

RATING.

COFFEE 4.75 / 5	🫘 🫘 🫘 🫘 🫘
OVERALL 4.75 / 5	★ ★ ★ ★ ★

Zibetto

1385 Sixth Avenue, Manhattan, NY 10019 | **Midtown East** ....

OPEN.

Mon-Fri.	7:00am - 7:00pm
Sat.	9:00am - 5:00pm
Sun.	10:00am - 4:00pm

This tiny, focused espresso bar was doing its thing before tiny, focused espresso bars were cool (since 2006). With barely enough room for a cello case, this is simply a coffee bar in the most literal sense. Zibetto roasts its own beans in Bologna and everything, from the service to the space, has a genuine contemporary Italian feel. Throw back a shot at the counter and get back to the Midtown grind.

FOOD.

A selection of Italian pastries from Milan-based Bindi Desserts.

CONTACT.

(917) 526-8112
www.zibettoespresso.com
info@zibetto.com
Subway F (57th St)

OVERVIEW.

Category
Independent
Owner
Anastasios Nougos
First opened
2006

COFFEE & EQUIPMENT.

Roaster
Zibetto
Machine
Brasilia Decurtis Camme
Grinder
Mazzer

PRICES.

Espresso	$2.00
Cappuccino	$3.50
Latte	$3.50

RATING.

COFFEE 4.00 / 5	🫘 🫘 🫘 🫘 🫘
OVERALL 4.00 / 5	★ ★ ★ ★ ★

"You can learn a technique, but you can only develop passion through dedication, love, pride, and respect for your work."

–La Marzocco co-founder, Piero Bambi

La Marzocco was founded in 1927 in Florence, Italy by two brothers, Guiseppe and Bruno Bambi. With a history rich in culture and innovation, La Marzocco has helped to build the specialty coffee community into a robust, quality-driven industry. Today, you will find La Marzocco espresso machines in many cafés around the world, offering customers the satisfaction expected from an industry leader.

FINE COFFEE MACHINES

SINCE 1927

La Marzocco

Upper Manhattan

From the Apollo Theatre in Harlem to the world-famous Metropolitan Museum of Art, northern Manhattan has a rich and varied cultural heritage. The Upper East Side boasts Museum Row, home to some of the greatest art and history museums in the country, as well as some of the best and most exclusive shopping in New York on Madison Avenue. The Upper West Side has a calmer feel, with the Lincoln Center for the Performing Arts and The Museum of Natural History. In between sits the vast Central Park, New York's beloved urban oasis.

Cafe Lalo

201 West 83rd Street, Manhattan, NY 10024 | Upper West Side ....

OPEN.

Mon-Thu.	8:00am - 2:00am
Fri.	8:00am - 4:00am
Sat.	9:00am - 4:00am
Sun.	Closed

This European-style café is a picturesque setting for a romantic espresso break. The cases of cakes, pies, cookies and tarts are impressively stocked and the coffee, supplied by the local Dallis Bros Coffee, is the perfect companion to a little (or a lot) of something sweet. During summer, the enormous front windows are pulled open, making this a charming spot to linger for a little while or into the wee small hours. When the sun is shining, enjoy a treat here, then take a stroll over to Central Park.

FOOD.

An impressive menu of cakes, pies, cookies and the like with an equally thorough menu of European-inspired brunch items, sandwiches, salads, egg dishes and small bites.

CONTACT.

(212) 496-6031
www.cafelalo.com
cafe@cafelalo.com
Subway 1, 2 (86th St)

OVERVIEW.

Category
Independent
Owner
Haim Lalo
First opened
1988

COFFEE & EQUIPMENT.

Roaster
Dallis Bros Coffee
Machine
Rancilio, 3 groups
Grinder
Fetco
Bulk brewer
Fetco

PRICES.

Filter / Drip	$2.00
Espresso	$2.50
Cappuccino	$3.75
Latte	$3.75

RATING.

COFFEE	3.50 / 5
OVERALL	4.25 / 5

Indian Road Cafe

600 West 218th Street, Manhattan, NY 10034 | **Inwood** ···

OPEN.

Mon-Thu.	7:00am - 10:30pm
Fri-Sat.	7:00am - 11:00pm
Sun.	8:00am - 10:00pm

This coffee bar located in the front of a restaurant is something of a coffee oasis for those above 100th Street. A constantly rotating menu of beans is served by baristas who are serious about providing a good coffee experience and many of them reside in the local area, contributing to the neighborhood feel. All coffee drinks are available to those dining at the restaurant, and most of the food menu is available at the coffee bar as well. Unlike most places in the city with coffee of this caliber, Indian Road Cafe feels natural, not art-directed, and you'll swear you're somewhere in the countryside, not an A-train ride away from Times Square.

FOOD.

A menu of fresh sandwiches and salads made with organic ingredients, and a vast array of American, French and Italian sweets.

CONTACT.

(212) 942-7451
indianroadcafe.com
Subway 1 (215th St) or A (Inwood - 207th St)

OVERVIEW.

Category
Independent
Owner
Jason Minter and Jason Berger
First opened
2008

COFFEE & EQUIPMENT.

Roaster
Counter Culture
Machine
La Marzocco GB/5
Grinder
Mazzer Super Jolly, Mazzer Major E, Bunn
Bulk brewer
Fetco

PRICES.

Filter / Drip	$2.00
Espresso	$2.25
Cappuccino	$3.25
Latte	$3.75

RATING.

COFFEE 4.00 / 5	🫘 🫘 🫘 🫘 🫘
OVERALL 4.00 / 5	★ ★ ★ ★ ☆

Joe Upper West Side

514 Columbus Avenue, Manhattan, NY 10024 | Upper West Side ....

OPEN.

Mon-Sat.	7:00am - 8:00pm
Sun.	8:00am - 8:00pm

OVERVIEW.

Category
Chain
Owner
Jonathan and Gabrielle Rubinstein
First opened
2009

COFFEE & EQUIPMENT.

Roaster
Ecco Coffee
Machine
La Marzocco GB/5
Grinder
Mazzer Robur E
Bulk brewer
Fetco

Plenty of sunlight soaks this Joe outpost on the Upper West Side, making it a particularly bright spot to grab a morning or afternoon coffee. Close to Central Park and The Museum of Natural History, Joe offers a pourover bar after noon and has a particularly knowledgeable and friendly staff of baristas who are always happy to talk through the offerings of the week. This is a small shop but a comfortable one, with a good deal of seating as well two handsome benches out front, where customers can watch the foot traffic down picturesque Columbus Avenue.

FOOD.

An assortment of cookies, muffins and other baked goods from Erica's Rugelach and Ceci Cela. Housemade baked goods are also made in partnership with Ovenly.

PRICES.

Filter / Drip	$2.25
Espresso	$2.50
Cappuccino	$3.75
Latte	$3.75

Other locations
Seven other locations in New York

CONTACT.

(212) 875-0100
www.joenewyork.com
joecoffeestore@gmail.com
Subway B, C (86th St)

RATING.

COFFEE 4.25 / 5	
OVERALL 4.25 / 5	★★★★⯪

Lenox Coffee

60 West 129th Street, Manhattan, NY 10027 | **Harlem** ....

OPEN.

Mon-Fri.	7:00am - 6:00pm
Sat-Sun.	8:00am - 6:00pm

Although it was opened with the goal of spreading third-wave coffee further uptown, this quiet shop recalls the romantic coffee houses of the 19th and 20th centuries. It's a modern update of the classic meeting place, but arguing intellectuals have now traded their notebooks for laptops. The antique decor is elegant and understated, with black-and-white photos of Paris adorning the walls, and the café itself is spacious and comfortable. The coffee is very good, with a drip that is light and floral, and the baristas serving it are always welcoming. This is a lovely spot to daydream about a New York that once was and, in places like this, maybe still is.

FOOD.

A small selection of sandwiches, granola, chocolate from Mast Brothers, bagels and baked goods from Balthazar and Ceci Cela.

CONTACT.

(617) 320-4788
www.lenoxcoffee.com
aaronbaird@lenoxcoffee.com
Subway 2, 3 (125th Street)

OVERVIEW.

Category
Independent
Owner
Aaron Baird and Jeffrey Green
First opened
2011

COFFEE & EQUIPMENT.

Roaster
Forty Ninth Parallel
Machine
La Marzocco Linea, 2 groups
Grinder
Kio Fresh
Bulk brewer
Fetco

PRICES.

Filter / Drip	$1.75
Espresso	$2.50
Cappuccino	$3.25
Latte	$3.25

RATING.

COFFEE	3.75 / 5
OVERALL	4.00 / 5

Oslo Upper East Side

442 East 75th Street, Manhattan, NY 10021 | **Upper East Side** ....

OPEN.

| **Mon-Fri.** | 7:00am - 6:00pm |
| **Sat-Sun.** | 8:00am - 6:00pm |

On a tree-lined side street off 1st Avenue, a molded metal door invites visitors to enter this Upper East Side outpost of Brooklyn coffee shop Oslo. This is a lovely neighborhood spot - small, friendly and bright with lots of sunlight and plenty of great coffee. The vintage lever espresso machine and the locally roasted beans are an awesome combination, with able hands pulling sweet and balanced lattes with ease and swiftness. Oslo is a welcome addition to the area and an easy choice when seeking a restorative beverage in this neck of the woods.

FOOD.

An assortment of cookies and muffins from Blue Sky as well as croissants from Ceci Cela Patisserie.

CONTACT.

(718) 782-0332
www.oslocoffee.com
info@oslocoffee.com
Subway 6 (77th St)

Other locations
Bedford Avenue / Roebling Street

OVERVIEW.

Category
Multi-independent
Owner
JD Merget and Kathy Merget
First opened
2011

COFFEE & EQUIPMENT.

Roaster
Oslo Coffee Roasters
Machine
Vintage San Marco Leva, 2 groups
Grinder
Mazzer
Bulk brewer
Bunn

PRICES.

Filter / Drip	$1.50
Espresso	$2.50
Cappuccino	$3.25
Latte	$3.25

RATING.

| COFFEE 4.25 / 5 | 🫘 🫘 🫘 🫘 🫘 |
| OVERALL 4.00 / 5 | ★ ★ ★ ★ ★ |

Untitled

945 Madison Avenue, Manhattan, NY 10021 | Upper East Side ....

OPEN.

Mon.	Closed
Tue-Thu.	8:00am - 3:00pm
Fri.	8:00am - 3:00pm, 6:00pm - 9:00pm
Sat Sun.	10:00am - 3:00pm, 6:00pm - 9:00pm

After touring the galleries of the Whitney Museum, take a trip downstairs to visit Danny Meyer's recently opened Untitled café. Chalkboards display the day's specials and the counter showcases various desserts and pies from local suppliers. Untitled's coffee of choice comes from Stumptown and is brewed to perfection by the café's baristas. As far as museum cafés go, Untitled offers an impressive array of breakfast, lunch and dinner options (although dinner is only offered Thursday to Saturday). Admission to the museum isn't necessary for a visit to Untitled, making this a coffee destination in its own right.

FOOD.

A New American menu offering soups, salads, sandwiches, entrees and brunch on the weekends, with pies from Four & Twenty Blackbirds, cakes from Betty Bakery and Blue Marble ice cream.

CONTACT.

(212) 570-3670
untitledatthewhitney.com
info@untitledatthewhitney.com
Subway 4, 6 (77th St)

OVERVIEW.

Category
Independent
Owner
Danny Meyer's Union Square Hospitality Group
First opened
2011

COFFEE & EQUIPMENT.

Roaster
Stumptown Coffee Roasters
Machine
La Marzocco Linea, 3 groups
Grinder
Mazzer
Bulk brewer
Fetco

PRICES.

Filter / Drip	$3.00
Espresso	$3.50
Cappuccino	$4.75
Latte	$4.75

RATING.

COFFEE 4.00 / 5

OVERALL 4.00 / 5

Park Slope & Surrounding

The largely residential neighborhoods of Bedford-Stuyvesant, Ditmas Park, Kensington, Prospect Heights and Park Slope encircle Prospect Park. Kensington and Ditmas Park still retain many examples of beautiful Victorian architecture, while Prospect Heights and Bed-Stuy are known for their rich cultural histories, with the Brooklyn Botanical Gardens, The Brooklyn Museum and The Pratt Institute all being found here. Park Slope itself, with its picturesque tree-lined streets, historic brownstones, popular restaurants and shops, is a great neighborhood to explore.

Bedford Hill Coffee Bar

343 Franklin Avenue, Brooklyn NY 11238 | Bed-Stuy

OPEN.

Sun-Tue.	7:00am - 6:00pm
Wed-Sat.	7:00am - midnight

A traditional coffee shop with a youthful twist, this Bed-Stuy café is a hidden treasure. Pop down the stairs and enjoy a bite, a nicely balanced (and reasonably priced) latte and the plentiful sunshine. Visit on a lazy Sunday morning with the newspaper or a couple of friends and spend an hour (or two) hanging out in this neighborhood shop. During the week, wifi is available for those seeking a more enjoyable place to work, but when evening comes, patrons are invited to put away their computers. Staff are always friendly and the shop's "buy a friend a coffee" chalkboard exemplifies the community atmosphere of this cute café.

FOOD.

Café fare such as salads, sandwiches, housemade baked goods and breakfast options.

CONTACT.

(718) 636-7650
bedfordhillbrooklyn.com
hi@bedfordhillbrooklyn.com
Subway G (Classon Ave), C (Franklin)

OVERVIEW.

Category
Independent
Owner
Allison Stuart
First opened
2010

COFFEE & EQUIPMENT.

Roaster
Anodyne Coffee Roasting Co
Machine
La Marzocco GB/5, 2 groups
Grinder
Mazzer Luigi

PRICES.

Espresso	$2.25
Cappuccino	$2.75
Latte	$2.75

RATING.

COFFEE 3.75 / 5

OVERALL 4.00 / 5

Breukelen Coffee House

764a Franklin Avenue, Brooklyn, NY 11238 | **Prospect Heights** ....

OPEN.

Mon-Fri.	7:00am - 7:00pm
Sat-Sun.	8:00am - 8:00pm

Good news: you don't have to move to Portland to find a spot that's fittingly grunge-chic because the 1990s are alive and well at Breukelen Coffee House. A loose, relaxed vibe pervades this Stumptown-serving shop. There's plenty of space to spread out and work, as well as opportunities to cross paths with local creatives. The Hair Bender espresso tends toward the strong and dark end of the spectrum, so if that's not quite your thing, go for a cortado instead. Many of the customers here are neighborhood regulars, but the baristas are friendly enough to make newcomers feel like one of the gang.

FOOD.

A selection of pastries from Ceci Cela bakery, as well as Terrace Bagels.

CONTACT.

(718) 789-7070
breukelencoffeehouse.com
info@breukelencoffeehouse.com
Subway 2, 3, 4, 5 (Franklin Ave)

OVERVIEW.

Category
Independent
Owner
Frank Warren
First opened
2009

COFFEE & EQUIPMENT.

Roaster
Stumptown Coffee Roasters
Machine
La Marzocco Linea
Grinder
Mazzer Major
Bulk brewer
Fetco

PRICES.

Filter / Drip	$1.75
Espresso	$2.50
Cappuccino	$3.25
Latte	$3.50

RATING.

COFFEE
3.75 / 5

OVERALL
4.00 / 5

Café Regular du Nord

158a Berkeley Place, Brooklyn, NY 11215 | Prospect Heights ....

This neighborhood café takes its cues from the needs of its locals; kid-friendly but definitely a place for grown-ups too, this Park Slope coffee bar is as delightful as it gets. The old New York feel of the antique interior gives Café Regular du Nord a sophisticated polish and the espresso here is made with elegance and skill to match. Add in after-school specials for kids (half-off pastries with a cup of hot chocolate) as well as discounts for teachers and students, and there's something for everyone at this beautiful little café.

FOOD.

Small snacks, cookies from Tumbador and pastries from the nearby Colson Patisserie.

CONTACT.

(718) 783-0673
www.caferegular.com
Subway B, Q (7th Ave) or 2, 3, 4 (Grand Army Plaza)

OPEN.

Mon-Sun. 7:00am - 6:00pm

OVERVIEW.

Category
Multi-independent
Owner
Anne Zavelo
First opened
2009

COFFEE & EQUIPMENT.

Roaster
La Colombe Torrefaction
Machine
La Spaziale, 2 groups
Grinder
La Spaziale
Bulk brewer
Bunn

PRICES.

Filter / Drip	$1.75
Espresso	$1.75
Cappuccino	$2.75
Latte	$2.75

Other locations
Park Slope

RATING.

COFFEE 3.75 / 5	
OVERALL 3.75 / 5	

Daily Press

505 Franklin Avenue, Brooklyn, NY 11238 | Bed-Stuy ....

OPEN.

Mon-Sat.	7:00am - 5:00pm
Sun.	8:00am - 6:00pm

Daily Press would be notable simply for being the only espresso bar in the area, but luckily for Bed-Stuy residents, it's also one of the brightest and most cheerful shops in the city. Recycled, weathered wood has transformed a former hair salon into a cozy, relaxed place to spend a morning. Friendly and well-trained baristas pull Intelligentsia espresso and French press is offered in lieu of bulk-brewed drip coffee.
The lattes and cappuccinos tend towards the milky end of the spectrum, so if that's not your thing, order a well-balanced cortado. A short list of single-origin pourovers is reliable and accessible.

FOOD.

Baked goods from Ceci Cela Patisserie and Terrance Bagels.

CONTACT.

(347) 240-1101
bedfordcornercafe@gmail.com
Subway A, C (Franklin Ave)

OVERVIEW.

Category
Independent
Owner
Michael Zawacki
First opened
2011

COFFEE & EQUIPMENT.

Roaster
Intelligentsia Coffee
Machine
La Marzocco - a custom hybrid of an FB/70 and an FB/80
Grinder
La Marzocco Swift

PRICES.

Filter / Drip	$2.25
Espresso	$2.75
Cappuccino	$4.50
Latte	$4.50

RATING.

COFFEE	
3.75 / 5	🫘🫘🫘🫘🫘
OVERALL	
4.25 / 5	★★★★⯪

98

De Luxe

410 7th Avenue, Brooklyn, NY 11215 | Park Slope ....

OPEN.

Mon.	Closed
Tue-Fri.	6:30am - 6:00pm
Sat.	7:30am - 7:00pm
Sun.	8:00am - 5:00pm

This mom-and-pop hipster shop is as adorable as it is delicious. A husband-and-wife team run this pint-sized coffee bar with ease and charm, and take pride in remembering the needs and whims of their regulars: the baby-toting parents and newspaper-reading gentlemen of Park Slope. This is a neighborhood shop, with a warm and welcoming feel and the subtle cool of a converted tattoo parlor. Stop in and enjoy an espresso made using DOMA beans roasted in Idaho, or maybe something heartier such as a fresh sandwich or fluffy doughnut.

FOOD.

Sandwiches and sweets from Balthazar, doughnuts from Dough on the weekends and other treats from This Chick Bakes.

CONTACT.

(718) 369-0601
deluxebrooklyn.com
andy or tina@deluxebrooklyn.com
Subway F, G (7th Ave)

OVERVIEW.

Category
Independent
Owner
Andy and Tina Schulz
First opened
2011

COFFEE & EQUIPMENT.

Roaster
DOMA Coffee Roasting Company
Machine
Faema E61, 2 groups
Grinder
Mazzer Major
Bulk brewer
Curtis GT

PRICES.

Filter / Drip	$1.75
Espresso	$1.75
Cappuccino	$3.50
Latte	$3.50

RATING.

COFFEE 3.75 / 5	
OVERALL 4.00 / 5	

Forty Weight Cafe

492 6th Avenue, Brooklyn, NY 11215 | **Park Slope** ....

OPEN.

Mon-Fri.	7:00am - 3:30pm
Sat-Sun.	8:00am - 3:30pm

Sharing a space with Sweet Wolf's restaurant, this Forty Weight Cafe is the flagship store for Forty Weight Coffee Roasters based in Ithaca, New York. This under-the-radar café boasts some of the best locally roasted coffee in the borough and at the pourover bar, you can try one of the company's single-origin roasts, which change regularly depending on the season. A carefully crafted espresso from one of the knowledgeable and friendly baristas is an equally good choice. The space is a little tight, with one long communal table as the main seating area, but it's worth the squeeze.

FOOD.

Sweet Wolf's provides gourmet sandwiches, burgers and plates. Forty Weight Cafe offers sweet and savory baked goods from Colson Patisserie, Margaret Palca Bakes and Sans Bakery.

CONTACT.

(718) 788-4926
www.fortyweightcoffee.com
matthew@fortyweightcoffee.com
Subway F, G (7th Ave)

OVERVIEW.

Category
Independent
Owner
Andrew Ballard and Matt Marks
First opened
2011

COFFEE & EQUIPMENT.

Roaster
Forty Weight Coffee Roasters
Machine
La Marzocco GB/5, 2 groups
Grinder
Mazzer Super Jolly, Ditting

PRICES.

Filter / Drip	$2.25
Espresso	$2.25
Cappuccino	$3.50
Latte	$4.00

RATING.

COFFEE 4.25 / 5	🫘 🫘 🫘 🫘 🫘
OVERALL 3.75 / 5	★ ★ ★ ★ ★

Glass Shop

766 Classon Avenue, Brooklyn, NY 11238 | **Prospect Heights** ....

This Australian-influenced shop is a gem for Prospect Heights dwellers and Brooklyn Museum visitors looking for serious coffee. Glass Shop has the distinction of being one of the first cafés in the city to offer a flat white, the stronger Australian version of a latte. Flat whites are a delight, but the espresso here is also plenty good to drink on its own. Come earlier in the day if you can, because the luscious housemade olive oil cake tends to sell out by mid-afternoon. Airy yet cozy, the space is adorned with cycling caps and imagery, Aussie condiments and a crate of oranges ready to be squeezed into juice. The highlight is the lush backyard decorated with antique doors, which acquires magical status during summer.

OPEN.

Mon-Fri.	8:00am - 6:00pm
Sat-Sun.	9:00am - 6:00pm

OVERVIEW.

Category
Independent
Owner
Francesco Agostino
and Catherine Weatherup
First opened
2009

COFFEE & EQUIPMENT.

Roaster
La Colombe Torrefaction
Machine
La Marzocco Linea
Grinder
Mazzer
Bulk brewer
Fetco

PRICES.

Filter / Drip	$2.00
Espresso	$2.50
Cappuccino	$3.25
Latte	$3.25

FOOD.
Housemade olive oil cake, muffins
and sandwiches.

CONTACT.
Subway 2, 3, 4, 5 (Franklin Ave)

RATING.

COFFEE
4.00 / 5

OVERALL
4.00 / 5

Gorilla Coffee

97 Fifth Avenue, Brooklyn, NY 11217 | **Park Slope** ·····································

One of the very first roasters in New York to go the specialty route, Gorilla Coffee still shines as one of the best. With carefully prepared coffee and a warm, dark vibe to the space, this Park Slope shop is a home away from home. Single origins are not only available on the Chemex during the day, but as espresso too, and tasting evenings allow customers to sample different single origins brewed using a variety of methods. For tea and pourover services, baristas will prepare a tray containing the cup and pot, along with the rest of your wonderful brew. It is also important to note that, although much depends on the mood of the baristas, Gorilla is a serious contender for the coffee shop with the best playlists in town.

PRICES.

Filter / Drip	$2.00
Espresso	$2.50
Cappuccino	$3.50
Latte	$3.50

FOOD.

An assortment of baked goods, pastries from Balthazar and muffins from Blue Sky.

CONTACT.

(718) 230-3244
gorillacoffee.com
info@gorillacoffee.com
Subway 2, 3, 4 (Bergen St) or D, N, R (Union St)

OPEN.

Mon-Sat.	7:00am - 9:00pm
Sun.	8:00am - 9:00pm

OVERVIEW.

Category
Independent
Owner
Darleen Scherer and Carol McLaughlin
First opened
2003

COFFEE & EQUIPMENT.

Roaster
Gorilla Coffee
Machine
Synesso Cyncra, 3 groups
Grinder
Mazzer Robur E
Bulk brewer
Fetco

RATING.

COFFEE
4.50 / 5

OVERALL
4.00 / 5

Konditori

186 Fifth Avenue, Brooklyn, NY 11217 | **Park Slope** ·······································

OPEN.

Mon-Fri.	7:00am - 8:00pm
Sat-Sun.	7:00am - 7:00pm

The Swedish word "konditori" translates as "where one goes for a coffee break" and this petite venue lives up to its name as a lovely place to do just that. Konditori uses its own beans, which are medium roasted in the traditional Swedish way. This light blend makes particularly refreshing cold brews but works just as well on the espresso machine. The atmosphere here is rustic and Konditori provides a bright and comfortable space to meet up with friends or work on your computer. The edible offerings are of special note, with such Swedish specialties as coco balls providing an excellent accompaniment to the coffee.

FOOD.

Baked goods from local purveyors, sandwiches, bagels and freshly made Swedish pastries such as coco balls and cardamom bread.

CONTACT.

(347) 384-2028
www.konditorinyc.com
info@konditorinyc.com
Subway D, N, R (Union St)

OVERVIEW.

Category
Multi-independent
Owner
Per Inglander and Ronny Kaj
First opened
2011

COFFEE & EQUIPMENT.

Roaster
Konditori house roast from a Brooklyn roastery
Machine
Nuova Simonelli
Grinder
Nuova Simonelli

PRICES.

Filter / Drip	$2.00
Espresso	$2.50
Cappuccino	$3.50
Latte	$3.50

Other locations
Allen Street

RATING.

COFFEE
4.25 / 5

OVERALL
4.00 / 5

Milk Bar

620 Vanderbilt Avenue, Brooklyn, NY 11238 | **Prospect Heights** ....

OPEN.

Mon-Fri.	7:30am - 6:00pm
Sat-Sun.	9:00am - 6:00pm

Perched on a sunny corner in Prospect Heights, this Aussie-inspired shop is a full service café with a menu focused on fresh, locally produced ingredients and favorites such as avocado toast and eggs and biscuits. Counter Culture single origins are offered, along with specialties such as flat whites and a decadent Australian iced coffee, consisting of chilled espresso served over vanilla ice cream with milk. The space is bright and airy, with polished wood and exposed brick walls that create the feel of a comfortable small-town shop. Milk Bar is a great choice for a lazy weekend brunch, particularly in warmer weather.

FOOD.

Australian café fare made with locally sourced ingredients whenever possible. Bread from Pain d'Avignon and milk from Battenkill Valley Creamery.

CONTACT.

(718) 230-0844
www.milkbarbrooklyn.com
milkbarbrooklyn@gmail.com
Subway 2, 3, 4 (Grand Army Plaza) or B, Q (7th Ave)

OVERVIEW.

Category
Independent
Owner
Alex Hall and Sabrina Godfrey
First opened
2009

COFFEE & EQUIPMENT.

Roaster
Counter Culture
Machine
La Marzocco Linea, 2 groups
Grinder
Mazzer, Bunn
Bulk brewer
Fetco

PRICES.

Filter / Drip	$2.00
Espresso	$2.50
Cappuccino	$3.50
Latte	$3.50

RATING.

COFFEE 4.25 / 5

OVERALL 4.00 / 5

Qathra

1112 Cortelyou Road, Brooklyn, NY 11218 | Ditmas Park

OPEN.
Mon-Sun.   7:00am - 9:00pm

The warm and friendly atmosphere at Qathra once and for all dispels the notion that a serious coffee shop need feel like an art gallery. A gem in quiet Ditmas Park (Park Slope's less highly strung younger sister), Qathra serves Counter Culture espresso alongside an extensive rotating pourover menu prepared by a staff of helpful baristas. A single visit might be enough to make Qathra your new neighborhood coffee shop - even if you have to step a little out of your way to pay a visit.

FOOD.

Pastries from Balthazar Bakery, as well as housemade breakfast items and sandwiches.

CONTACT.

(718) 484-3322
www.qathracafe.com
qathracafe@yahoo.com
Subway Q (Cortelyou Rd)

OVERVIEW.

Category
Independent
Owner
Max Habib
First opened
2010

COFFEE & EQUIPMENT.

Roaster
Counter Culture
Machine
La Marzocco Strada MP
Grinder
Mazzer Robur E
Bulk brewer
Fetco

PRICES.

Filter / Drip	$1.75
Espresso	$2.50
Cappuccino	$3.50
Latte	$4.00

RATING.

COFFEE 4.50 / 5	🫘🫘🫘🫘🫘
OVERALL 4.25 / 5	★★★★⯪

Root Hill Cafe

262 Fourth Avenue, Brooklyn, NY 11215 | **Park Slope** ....

OPEN.

Mon-Thu.	7:30am - 7:30pm
Sat.	8:00am - 7:00pm
Sun.	8:30am - 6:00pm

Ideally located in Park Slope, this bright café is a hub for this burgeoning trendy neighborhood. Depending on what time of day it is, the vibe here oscillates between tranquil or bustling, and the service between hospitable or efficient. The Dallis Bros espresso is roasted in Brooklyn and is rich and smooth, with a flavor that doesn't overstay its welcome. The freshly baked peanut-butter-and-jelly cookies are some the best you'll ever have. Order a cortado, perch yourself on a stool facing the street and watch the neighborhood grow.

OVERVIEW.

Category
Independent
Owner
Maria Bowen, Michelle Giancola, Andrew Giancola and Stephen Kelley
First opened
2008

COFFEE & EQUIPMENT.

Roaster
Dallis Bros Coffee
Machine
La Marzocco GB/5
Grinder
Mazzer Major
Bulk brewer
Fetco

FOOD.

A full menu of breakfast and lunch comfort food entrees, alongside housemade baked goods.

PRICES.

Filter / Drip	$1.75
Espresso	$2.50
Cappuccino	$3.25
Latte	$3.50

CONTACT.

(718) 797-0100
www.roothillcafe.com
roothill@gmail.com
Subway R (Union St)

Other locations
Root Hill Burger

RATING.

COFFEE 4.00 / 5	
OVERALL 4.00 / 5	

Roots Café

639 Fifth Avenue, Brooklyn, NY 11215 | **Park Slope** ....

OPEN.

Mon-Thu.	6:30am - 8:00pm
Fri.	6:30am - 10:30pm
Sat.	7:30am - 8:00pm
Sun.	8:30am - 8:00pm

It's all about "coffee, community and culture" here at Roots Café, as owner Jamey Hamm says. The coffee may be from Stumptown's Brooklyn roastery, but the vibe at this snug Park Slope shop is straight from the South, with a kind of hospitality and easy comfort that's recognizable the moment you step through the door. Roots offers laidback housemade food with vegan, vegetarian and gluten-free options, but although the shop may have a relaxed feel, the coffee drinks here are made at an appropriately New York speed. Roots is a popular neighborhood haunt that often hosts musical events and art exhibitions at which local musicians, artists and friends can usually be seen joining in the revelry.

FOOD.

An extensive menu of vegetarian, vegan and gluten-free offerings such as sandwiches and wraps, as well as baked goods from Blue Sky Bakery.

CONTACT.

rootscafebrooklyn.blogspot.com
info@rootscafebrooklyn.com
Subway D, N, R (Prospect Ave)

OVERVIEW.

Category
Independent
Owner
Jamey Hamm
First opened
2008

COFFEE & EQUIPMENT.

Roaster
Stumptown Coffee Roasters
Machine
La Marzocco Linea, 2 groups
Grinder
Swift, Bunn
Bulk brewer
Fetco

PRICES.

Filter / Drip	$1.50
Espresso	$2.25
Cappuccino	$3.50
Latte	$4.00

RATING.

COFFEE 4.00 / 5	🫘 🫘 🫘 🫘 🫘
OVERALL 4.00 / 5	★ ★ ★ ★ ★

Sit & Wonder

688 Washington Avenue, Brooklyn, NY 11238 | **Prospect Heights** ....

OPEN.

Mon-Fri.	7:00am - 7:00pm
Sat-Sun.	8:00am - 7:00pm

With stained-glass lamps, a polished wooden bar and a charmingly mismatched set of chairs and sofas, this spot is a quiet and modestly elegant place to take a break. The vibe is quirky and the coffee is as reasonably priced as it is flavorful. A small drip is only $1.25, a steal for an artisan coffee shop, and free coffee tasting is offered to patrons from 4pm on Wednesdays. When the weather is good, venture out into the garden at the back of the café to enjoy your cold-brewed coffee in the sun.

FOOD.

Fresh sandwiches, granola and baked goods from local bakeries.

CONTACT.

(718) 622-0299
sitandwonder.org
info@sitandwonder.org
Subway A, C (Franklin Ave) or 2, 3, 4 (Eastern Parkway - Brooklyn Museum)

OVERVIEW.

Category
Independent
Owner
Fernando Aciar
First opened
2011

COFFEE & EQUIPMENT.

Roaster
Stumptown Coffee Roasters
Machine
La Marzocco FB/80
Grinder
Swift, Bunn
Bulk brewer
Fetco

PRICES.

Filter / Drip	$1.25
Espresso	$2.50
Cappuccino	$3.00
Latte	$3.25

RATING.

COFFEE 4.00 / 5	🫘🫘🫘🫘🫘
OVERALL 4.00 / 5	★★★★★

Southside Coffee

652 6th Avenue, Brooklyn, NY 11215 | **Park Slope** ....

OPEN.

Mon-Fri.	7:00am - 6:00pm
Sat-Sun.	8:00am - 6:00pm

A straightforward café with a serious coffee focus, Southside supplies superior drinks with an uncomplicated attitude. The space is small and basic, with some tables, chairs and a sofa in the back, which reflects Southside's simple approach to coffee - just make the best that's out there. This is a small operation where the owners run the shop themselves, pulling shots and grabbing pastries from their sister establishment, Lot 2, across the street. A rotating menu of roasters including Counter Culture and Coava is offered, and the espressos here are sweet and full-bodied. With all these elements combined, Southside Coffee shines, plain and simple.

FOOD.

A small selection of baked goods is made across the street at Lot 2, Southside's sister restaurant.

CONTACT.

(347) 599-0887
Subway D, N, R (Prospect Ave)

Other locations
Lot 2

OVERVIEW.

Category
Independent
Owner
Ben Jones, Joshua Sidis
and Amber Sather
First opened
January 2009

COFFEE & EQUIPMENT.

Roaster
Counter Culture, George Howell Coffee
(Alchemy Espresso), Coava, PT's
and others
Machine
La Marzocco GB/5
Grinder
Mazzer

PRICES.

Filter / Drip	$1.75
Espresso	$2.50
Cappuccino	$3.50
Latte	$3.75

RATING.

COFFEE	
4.00 / 5	
OVERALL	
3.75 / 5	

Steeplechase

3013 Fort Hamilton Parkway, Brooklyn, NY 11218 | **Kensington** ....

OPEN.

Mon-Fri.	7:00am - 7:00pm
Sat-Sun.	8:00am - 7:00pm

When Steeplechase owners Lynn and Keith McKee moved from Park Slope to Kensington, they were dismayed to find no serious coffee shops in their new neighborhood. So they did what all sensible people would do and opened one. Steeplechase eschews drip coffee in favor of French press and (well-priced) pourovers, which you can enjoy at one of a few small tables. The Brooklyn Roasting Company espresso rotates regularly and is sure to impress.

FOOD.

Pastries from Trois Pommes Bakery and Balthazar Bakery.

CONTACT.

(347) 799-2640

www.steeplechasecoffee.com

Subway F,G (Fort Hamilton Pkwy)

OVERVIEW.

Category
Independent
Owner
Lynn McKee and Keith McKee
First opened
2011

COFFEE & EQUIPMENT.

Roaster
Brooklyn Roasting Company
Machine
La Marzocco Linea MP
Grinder
Mazzer Major

PRICES.

Filter / Drip	$1.50
Espresso	$2.50
Cappuccino	$3.50
Latte	$3.75

Hario V60 is offered on a drip bar custom-made by co-owner Keith McKee

RATING.

COFFEE
4.00 / 5

OVERALL
3.75 / 5

Downtown Brooklyn

With The Brooklyn Academy of Music in Fort Greene, the beautiful and historic Promenade along the water in Brooklyn Heights and all the fashionable shops and restaurants in Carroll Gardens and Cobble Hill, it's easy to wander a day away in Downtown Brooklyn. These largely residential areas are filled with beautiful tree-lined streets and quiet parks, and are known for being home to many of New York's greatest artists, writers and musicians.

Cafe Pedlar

210 Smith Street, Brooklyn, NY 11201 | **Cobble Hill** ....

OPEN.
Mon-Sun.   7:00am - 7:00pm

The renowned chefs behind the trio of Frankies Spuntino restaurants across New York City opened this artisan coffee shop in 2009. The café is small but feels much bigger, as the seating is spread out and the large windows invite plenty of sun. Some of the baked goods are made fresh at Pedlar's own bakery, The Bake Shop at Frankies Spuntino, and the coffee beans come fresh from the local Stumptown roastery in Red Hook. The café also has a small general store rack displaying coffee-making supplies, extra virgin olive oil and other gourmet goodies. Wander around this charming little neighborhood and grab a single-origin espresso and a pretzel braid for a simple, delicious afternoon snack.

OVERVIEW.

Category
Independent
Owner
Frank Castronovo and Frank Falcinelli
First opened
2009

COFFEE & EQUIPMENT.

Roaster
Stumptown Coffee Roasters
Machine
La Marzocco GB/5
Grinder
Mazzer
Bulk brewer
Fetco

FOOD.

An assortment of sweet and savory bites and baked goods, some made at Pedlar's own bake shop, others from local purveyors such as Blue Sky Bakery.

PRICES.

Filter / Drip	$2.00
Espresso	$2.50
Cappuccino	$3.75
Latte	$4.00

CONTACT.

(718) 855-7129
www.cafepedlar.com
info@cafepedlar.com
Subway F, G (Bergen St)

RATING.

COFFEE
4.00 / 5

OVERALL
4.00 / 5

Clover's Fine Art Gallery & Cafe

338 Atlantic Avenue, Brooklyn, NY 11201 | **Boerum Hill** ....

OPEN.
Wed-Sun.   12:00pm - 6:00pm

This Brooklyn gallery is a sweet surprise, offering a particularly cultured cup of coffee on busy Atlantic Avenue. Art and coffee blends together as seamlessly as the lattes here and you'll feel almost as stylish and refined as the decor as you sip an espresso before wandering through the gallery. Wifi is offered in the front area along with the drinks and some small bites such as fresh Jamaican patties and paninis. Exhibitions showcase work by artists from Brooklyn to Trinidad and beyond, so stop by and drink in everything this place has to offer.

FOOD.

A small menu of bites such as fresh Jamaican patties, sweets and baked goods.

CONTACT.

(718) 625-2121
www.cloversfineart.com
clover@cloversfineart.com
Subway F, G, (Bergen St) or A, C, G
(Hoyt - Schermerhorn)

OVERVIEW.

Category
Independent
Owner
Clover Barrett
First opened
2009

COFFEE & EQUIPMENT.

Roaster
Intelligentsia Coffee, Jamaican Blue Mountain Coffee from Coffee Traders Ltd
Machine
La Marzocco FB/80
Grinder
Mahlkönig
Bulk brewer
Clover

PRICES.

Filter / Drip	$3.00
Espresso	$2.75
Cappuccino	$3.25
Latte	$3.75

RATING.

COFFEE	
4.00 / 5	🫘🫘🫘🫘🫘
OVERALL	
4.00 / 5	★★★★★

Crop to Cup

541 3rd Avenue, Brooklyn, NY 11215 | Gowanus ······························

Crop to Cup has installed a small coffee bar at the front of its offices and in doing so created a mecca for coffee geeks. Only a sheer curtain separates the public from the Crop to Cup masterminds, so if you're lucky, you'll see them in action, comparing tasting notes or sampling prospective beans. In the meantime your knowledgeable barista will guide you through the pourover menu, one of the most extensive and reasonably priced in town. The espresso drinks are equally remarkable: complex, flavorful and remarkably inexpensive.

OPEN.
Mon-Sat.   8:00am - 5:30pm
Sun.   9:00am - 5:00pm

OVERVIEW.
Category
Chain
Owner
Taylor Mork
First opened
2011

COFFEE & EQUIPMENT.
Roaster
Crop to Cup
Machine
Rancilio Classe 6
Grinder
Mazzer Major

Other locations
Brooklyn Flea

PRICES.
Filter / Drip	$2.00
Espresso	$2.00
Cappuccino	$3.00
Latte	$3.00

FOOD.
A snack of bread and jam from Bien Cuit bakery is offered.

CONTACT.
(917) 531-8754
www.croptocup.com
c2cbrewbar@gmail.com
Subway F,G (4th Ave)

RATING.

COFFEE
4.25 / 5

OVERALL
4.00 / 5

118

Iris Cafe

20 Columbia Place, Brooklyn, NY 11201 | **Brooklyn Heights** ....

Tucked away on a quiet, historic street, Iris Cafe is a gloriously charming Brooklyn Heights spot. As off the beaten path as it is, this café gets packed on the weekends, and serves excellent Stumptown coffee and absurdly delicious gourmet sandwiches, salads and baked goods to the masses. The focus is on traditional recipes and ingredients (such as maple syrup instead of sugar) that are wholesome and don't compromise on taste. The food is exceptional and the French Dip is of particular note, with a jus prepared using brewed coffee and a touch of Manhattan Special, an espresso coffee soda that has been a Brooklyn institution for more than 100 years. Espresso drinks are well pulled and deeply satisfying, making ideal accompaniments to the lovely café fare.

OPEN.

Mon-Fri.	8:00am - 10:00pm
Sat- Sun.	8:00am - 5:00pm

OVERVIEW.

Category
Independent
Owner
Rachel Graville and Salah Hamdan
First opened
2010

COFFEE & EQUIPMENT.

Roaster
Stumptown Coffee Roasters,
Handsome Coffee Roasters,
Intelligentsia and others
Machine
La Marzocco GB/5
Grinder
Mazzer Kony, Mazzer Major
Bulk brewer
Fetco

Other locations
16 Columbia Place

PRICES.

Filter / Drip	$1.75
Espresso	$2.25
Cappuccino	$3.50
Latte	$4.25

FOOD.

A full menu of homemade sandwiches and baked goods, all made in house, except breads from Il Forno, Pain D'Avignon and Everybody Eats!

CONTACT.

(718) 722-7395
iriscafenyc.com
inquiries@iriscafenyc.com
Subway 2, 3, 4, 5 (Borough Hall) or N, R (Court St)

RATING.

COFFEE
4.25 / 5

OVERALL
4.50 / 5 ★★★★⯪

Smith Canteen

343 Smith Street, Brooklyn, NY 11231 | **Carroll Gardens** ....

This is the kind of café that can make you want to drop everything, find the nearest realtor and move into the neighborhood. Housed in a bright and welcoming space that was formerly a neighborhood pharmacy, Smith is committed to local sourcing and environmental awareness. This is reflected in its choice to serve coffee by Counter Culture, a company that prides itself on sustainability. For much of the day, Smith is usually too busy to linger at for long, but despite the turnover, it never loses its tranquil atmosphere. Those reluctantly confined to decaf can finally overcome their inferiority complex with a Smith specialty - the chickory latte. Made with powdered lettuce-root, it's a rich, flavorful beverage that succeeds on its own terms.

OPEN.
Mon-Sun.   7:00am - 6:00pm

OVERVIEW.
Category
Independent
Owner
Rob Newton
First opened
2011

COFFEE & EQUIPMENT.
Roaster
Counter Culture
Machine
La Marzocco Linea
Grinder
Mazzer
Bulk brewer
Fetco

PRICES.
Filter / Drip	$2.00
Espresso	$2.00
Cappuccino	$4.00
Latte	$4.00

FOOD.
A full breakfast and lunch menu, with housemade baked goods too.

CONTACT.
(718) 422-0444
www.smithcanteen.com
Subway F, G (Carroll St)

RATING.
COFFEE 4.50 / 5
OVERALL 4.50 / 5

Van Leeuwen

81 Bergen Street, Brooklyn, NY 11217 | **Boerum Hill** ....

OPEN.

Mon-Thu.	7:00am - 11:00pm
Fri.	7:00am - midnight
Sat.	9:00am - midnight
Sun.	9:00am - 11:00pm

An ice cream shop with a smart coffee instinct, this sun-soaked café features Intelligentsia espresso and some of the best gourmet ice cream in the city. Van Leeuwen's cold-brewed coffee is a sweet and refreshing revelation, but if you're really smart, you'll indulge in an affogato, a scoop of vanilla ice cream covered in espresso. The shop itself is bright and airy, with a simple, floral interior and classic tunes playing on the record player. This is a great spot for a cute date or to take the kids for a scoop after school, and maybe treat yourself to a little something too.

FOOD.

Artisanal ice cream, fresh waffles, housemade baked goods and savory items.

CONTACT.

(347) 763 2979
www.vanleeuwenicecream.com
hello@vanleeuwenicecream.com
Subway F, G (Bergen St)

Other locations

632 Manhattan Avenue / 48 1/2 East 7th Street / Madison Square / Bedford Avenue / Greenwich Village

OVERVIEW.

Category
Multi-independent
Owner
Laura O'Neill, Ben Van Leeuwen and Pete Van Leeuwen
First opened
2011

COFFEE & EQUIPMENT.

Roaster
Intelligentsia Coffee
Machine
Kees van der Westen Mirage Veloce, 2 groups
Grinder
Mazzer Major, Mazzer Minor
Bulk brewer
Fetco

PRICES.

Filter / Drip	$1.50
Espresso	$2.25
Cappuccino	$3.50
Latte	$4.00

RATING.

COFFEE	4.00 / 5
OVERALL	4.25 / 5

WTF Coffee Lab

47 Willoughby Avenue, Brooklyn, NY 11205 | Fort Greene ································

OPEN.
Mon-Sun.   7:00am - 7:00pm

Get your geek on and experiment with your coffee of choice at this Fort Greene spot, where a multitude of brewing options and a menu of at least six different single origins are on offer at any given time. Every cup is made to order at this chill coffee lab, where you'll find some mean espresso and an extensive drip bar featuring such methods as V60, Chemex and Sock Pot. It's small but sleek, with Kyoto towers lining the walls, giving the space that scientific feel. Coffee comes from Coava and PT's and the baristas will happily talk you through what's on the bar so you can pick the right cup for you. Try something new, maybe the Uganda peaberry on a siphon? All the cool kids are doing it.

OVERVIEW.
Category
Independent
Owner
Asio Highsmith
First opened
2010

COFFEE & EQUIPMENT.
Roaster
Coava and PT's
Machine
La Marzocco GB/5, 3 groups
Grinder
Mazzer Luigi

PRICES.
Filter / Drip	$4.00
Espresso	$3.00
Cappuccino	$3.75
Latte	$4.00

FOOD.
Granola and oatmeal in the mornings, with a small menu of pastries from Balthazar, as well as smoothies during the day.

Single-origin espresso changes daily and beans are rotated each month

CONTACT.
wtfcoffeelaboratory.com
wtfcoffeelaboratory@gmail.com
Subway G (Clinton - Washington Aves) and A, C (Lafayette Ave)

RATING.

COFFEE
4.50 / 5

OVERALL
4.00 / 5

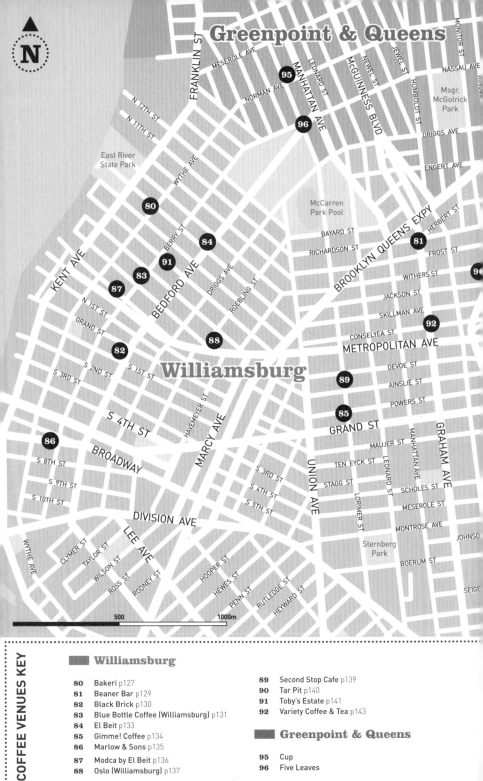

N

N 12TH ST
N 11TH ST

FRANKLIN ST

MESEROLE AVE

NORMAN AVE

LEONARD ST

MANHATTAN AVE

MCGUINNESS BLVD

NEWEL ST

JEWEL ST

MONITOR ST

NASSAU AVE

Msgr.
McGolrick
Park

DRIGGS AVE

ENGERT AVE

East River
State Park

WYTHE AVE

McCarren
Park Pool

BAYARD ST

RICHARDSON ST

BROOKLYN QUEENS EXPY

HERBERT ST

FROST ST

WITHERS ST

JACKSON ST

SKILLMAN AVE

CONSELYEA ST

METROPOLITAN AVE

DEVOE ST

AINSLIE ST

POWERS ST

KENT AVE

N 1ST ST

GRAND ST

BEDFORD AVE

BERRY ST

DRIGGS AVE

ROEBLING ST

HAVEMEYER ST

MARCY AVE

Williamsburg

S 2ND ST
S 1ST ST
S 3RD ST

S 4TH ST

BROADWAY

S 8TH ST

S 9TH ST

S 10TH ST

DIVISION AVE

WYTHE AVE

CLYMER ST

TAYLOR ST

WILSON ST

ROSS ST

RODNEY ST

LEE AVE

HOOPER ST

HEWES ST

PENN ST

RUTLEDGE ST

HEYWARD ST

S 3RD ST

S 4TH ST

S 5TH ST

UNION AVE

GRAND ST

MAUJER ST

TEN EYCK ST

STAGG ST

SCHOLES ST

MESEROLE ST

MONTROSE AVE

BOERUM ST

LORIMER ST

LEONARD ST

MANHATTAN AVE

GRAHAM AVE

Sternberg
Park

JOHNSO

SEIGE

80
84
91
83
87
82
88
86
89
85
81
92
95
96

500   1000m

Williamsburg

Williamsburg is a popular, trendy neighborhood with a lively, youthful feel. This area is a mecca for foodies, with lots of coffee roasteries housed in its converted warehouses, the Smorgasburg food market on the waterfront in the summertime and plenty of exciting restaurants. It's also home to a range of vintage shops, art galleries, music venues and McCarren Park on its northern edge.

Bakeri

150 Wythe Avenue, Brooklyn, NY 11211 | **Williamsburg** ·······································

This delightful little bakery offers both excellent coffee and splendid baked goods, all of which are made on site, from delicious tartines to magnificent cakes and pastries. The space is petite but cozy and antique details such as the marble countertop and painted tin ceiling make Bakeri a sweet place to settle for an hour. When the weather permits, the backyard patio is a particularly charming spot to sip a latte and indulge in one or two tempting treats.

OPEN.
Mon-Sun.   8:00am - 7:00pm

OVERVIEW.
Category
Independent
Owner
Nina Brondmo
First opened
2009

COFFEE & EQUIPMENT.
Roaster
Counter Culture
Machine
La Marzocco Linea
Grinder
Mazzer Luigi
Bulk brewer
Fetco

PRICES.
Filter / Drip	$1.50
Espresso	$2.25
Cappuccino	$3.50
Latte	$3.50

FOOD.
A extensive menu of housemade
pastries, cookies, cakes, pies,
sandwiches and small plates.
Wonderful artisan breads baked
in house.

CONTACT.
(718) 388-8037
www.bakeribrooklyn.com
info@bakeribrooklyn.com
Subway L (Bedford Ave)

RATING.

COFFEE
4.00 / 5

OVERALL
4.00 / 5

Beaner Bar

447 Graham Avenue, Brooklyn, NY 11211 | **Williamsburg** ·······························

Mon-Fri.	7:30am - 7:00pm
Sat-Sun.	8:30am - 7:00pm

This tiny Mexican coffee bar at the far end of Graham Avenue puts an inventive spin on the concept of the artisan New York coffee shop. With such house specialties as the Mexican Mocha (made with hand-ground Mexican chocolate mixed with spices and espresso), fresh tamales and more familiar offerings such as scones, cookies and a drip bar, this shop is a true original. The space is small with only a few seats at the counter and staff are always welcoming. Grab your cup to go and check out the shops and Italian specialty stores that line the street.

FOOD.

Fresh tamales and an assortment of baked goods from neighborhood bakeries such as Champs, Him in the Kitchen and Luminous Kitchen.

CONTACT.

www.beanerbar.com
beanerbar@gmail.com
Subway L (Graham Ave)

OVERVIEW.

Category
Independent
Owner
Lori Erlitz, Veronica Trevino and Rudy De La Rosa
First opened
2008

COFFEE & EQUIPMENT.

Roaster
Counter Culture
Machine
La Marzocco Linea, 3 groups
Grinder
Mazzer
Bulk brewer
Fetco

PRICES.

Filter / Drip	$1.60
Espresso	$2.70
Cappuccino	$3.55
Latte	$4.10

RATING.

COFFEE	
4.25 / 5	🫘🫘🫘🫘🫘
OVERALL	
4.00 / 5	★★★★★

Black Brick

300 Bedford Avenue, Brooklyn, NY 11211 | **Williamsburg** ....

OPEN.

Mon-Fri.	7:00am - 8:00pm
Sat-Sun.	8:00am - 8:00pm

Black Brick is the quintessential third-wave coffee shop done right. With an Americana-themed interior featuring a hand-built ceiling made from 300 crates and a plethora of quirky tchotchkes gathered from all over the country, this place is a great spot to stop in for a cup. The only thing that isn't vintage here is the coffee, which is fresh, bright and slightly sweet. With coffee like this, free wifi and that down-home, kitschy atmosphere, this café is a happy addition to a neighborhood that has established itself as a serious coffee district.

FOOD.
Croissants, both sweet and savory.

CONTACT.
(718) 384-0075
Subway L (Bedford Ave)

OVERVIEW.
Category
Independent
Owner
Kal Ali
First opened
2011

COFFEE & EQUIPMENT.
Roaster
Stumptown Coffee Roasters
Machine
La Marzocco Linea, 3 groups
Grinder
Mazzer Robur E

PRICES.

Filter / Drip	$1.50
Espresso	$2.50
Cappuccino	$3.50
Latte	$3.75

RATING.

COFFEE	4.00 / 5
OVERALL	4.00 / 5

Blue Bottle Coffee Williamsburg

160 Berry Street, Brooklyn, NY 11211 | **Williamsburg** ....

Blue Bottle is an American coffee institution and this, its first New York outpost, demonstrates why. The coffee here is powerfully delicious, with each cup carefully prepared by knowledgeable baristas, and the housemade pastries are out of this world. The double chocolate cookie, baked with Mast Brothers chocolate (made only a few blocks away), may change your life, along with everything else in this inventive and exciting shop. Blue Bottle feels more like a laboratory than a café at times, in the very best sense. Watch the Kyoto towers drip or take a peek at the back of the space where the roasting magic happens. When the sun is shining, grab an addictive cold-brewed New Orleans coffee and take a stroll along the waterfront (and maybe snag one of those cookies while you're at it).

OPEN.

Mon-Fri.	7:00am - 7:00pm
Sat-Sun.	8:00am - 7:00pm

OVERVIEW.

Category
Chain
Owner
James Freeman
First opened
2010

COFFEE & EQUIPMENT.

Roaster
Blue Bottle Coffee, with beans roasted fresh in house
Machine
La Marzocco FB/80 and a restored 1958 Faema Urania
Grinder
Nuova Simonelli, Mazzer

Other locations
Chelsea / Rockefeller Center / Highline (summer only)

PRICES.

Filter / Drip	$2.75
Espresso	$2.75
Cappuccino	$3.50
Latte	$4.00

FOOD.

A small assortment of treats, both savory and sweet, all lovingly prepared in house and with organic and locally produced ingredients.

CONTACT.

(718) 387-4160
www.bluebottlecoffee.net
info@bluebottlecoffee.net
Subway L (Bedford Ave)

RATING.

COFFEE	4.75 / 5
OVERALL	4.75 / 5

El Beit

154 Bedford Avenue, Brooklyn, NY 11211 | **Williamsburg** ....

OPEN.

Mon-Fri.	7:00am - 10:00pm
Sat-Sun.	8:00am - 11:00pm

Conveniently located on bustling Bedford Avenue, El Beit is nestled among the vintage shops, boutiques and gourmet eateries on this popular strip. Thanks to a rotating menu of single-origin beans from Forty Ninth Parallel, the coffee here is dependably great, and the backyard patio is the perfect spot to enjoy it. Baked goods are prepared fresh at El Beit's sister shop Modca, only a few blocks away, making this a wonderfully well-rounded café and a perfect spot to visit before venturing out to explore the neighborhood.

FOOD.

Freshly baked goods such as muffins, cookies and loaves prepared at sister shop Modca.

CONTACT.

(718) 302-1810
Subway L (Bedford Ave)

Other locations
Modca

OVERVIEW.

Category
Independent
Owner
Bassam Ali
First opened
2008

COFFEE & EQUIPMENT.

Roaster
Forty Ninth Parallel
Machine
La Marzocco FB/70
Grinder
Anfim, Ditting
Bulk brewer
Fetco, Clover

PRICES.

Filter / Drip	$2.00
Espresso	$2.50
Cappuccino	$3.75
Latte	$4.00

RATING.

COFFEE 4.00 / 5	🫘 🫘 🫘 🫘 🫘
OVERALL 4.00 / 5	★ ★ ★ ★ ★

Gimme! Coffee

495 Lorimer Street, Brooklyn, NY 11211 | **Williamsburg** ....

Home to some of New York's most passionate coffee fanatics, Gimme! means business. Here coffee is more than a drink - it's a lifestyle choice, one that brings joy, focus and deliciousness to all. The baristas here are intensely intelligent about all coffee-related matters and will happily guide customers through any dilemma, whether it be what beans will work best with your preferred brewing method or what single origin to order at the bar. The space is simple and minimal, which focuses attention on the top-quality coffee.

FOOD.
Cookies from This Chick Bakes, pastries from Ceci Cela, doughnuts from Dough and biscotti from Krums Corners.

CONTACT.
(718) 388-7771
www.gimmecoffee.com
Subway L (Lorimer St) or G (Metropolitan Ave)

OPEN.
Mon-Sun.   7:00am - 7:30pm

OVERVIEW.
Category
Chain
Owner
Kevin Cuddeback
First opened
2003

COFFEE & EQUIPMENT.
Roaster
Gimme! Coffee
Machine
La Marzocco GB/5, 3 groups
Grinder
Mazzer Robur E
Bulk brewer
Bunn

PRICES.
Filter / Drip	$1.50
Espresso	$2.25
Cappuccino	$3.50
Latte	$3.75

Other locations
Soho / Williamsburg

RATING.

COFFEE 4.50 / 5

OVERALL 4.25 / 5

Marlow & Sons

81 Broadway, Brooklyn, NY 11249 | **Williamsburg** ....

OPEN.

Mon-Sun.   8:00am - 4:00pm,
                5:00pm - midnight

Marlow & Sons has no interest in being a great restaurant that also happens to serve coffee; instead it is as remarkable as a coffee shop as it is a restaurant. The space speaks to this with a front room that is equipped with a full, bustling coffee bar run by fanatical baristas. Resembling a general store that sells artisanal groceries such as Wheelhouse Pickles, the pale blue room has a few tables to perch at and all coffee beverages are available in the main restaurant, which has a warm, secluded lodge atmosphere. Coffee beans are sourced from a rotating groups of roasteries, with freshness being of paramount importance. This a spot that's worth going out of your way to discover.

FOOD.

Full restaurant menu served out the back, with a large selection of housemade baked goods offered out the front.

CONTACT.

(718) 384-1441
www.marlowandsons.com
contact@marlowandsons.com
Subway L (Bedford Ave), J, M, Z (Marcy Ave)

OVERVIEW.

Category
Independent
Owner
Andrew Tarlow
First opened
2004

COFFEE & EQUIPMENT.

Roaster
Terroir Select, Four Barrel Coffee and Sightglass
Machine
La Marzocco Linea
Grinder
Mazzer Robur E

PRICES.

Filter / Drip	$2.00
Espresso	$2.75
Cappuccino	$3.50
Latte	$4.00

RATING.

COFFEE
4.25 / 5

OVERALL
4.25 / 5

Modca by El Beit

103 North 3rd Street, Brooklyn, NY 11249 | Williamsburg ·····················

OPEN.

Mon-Sat.	7:30am - 8:00pm
Sun.	8:30am - 8:00pm

The space at Modca feels like a country attic built inside a former warehouse, which might seem antithetical, but is remarkably fitting for a café in Williamsburg. The sense of coziness that is achieved within an industrial framework results in a café that is both comfortable and spacious, and plenty of tables are available at which to meet a friend or focus on some work. The baristas here are friendly, helpful and skilled, providing perfectly balanced espresso drinks and great cold-brewed coffee for hot days. Single origins are offered as pourovers and lots of tempting edibles such as banana loaf and M&M Monster cookies are available if eyes wander towards the pastry case.

FOOD.

An abundance of baked goods made fresh in the café.

CONTACT.

(718) 387-2406
Subway L (Bedford Ave)

OVERVIEW.

Category
Independent
Owner
Bassam Ali
First opened
2011

COFFEE & EQUIPMENT.

Roaster
Forty Ninth Parallel
Machine
La Marzocco Mistral, 3 groups
Grinder
Anfim

PRICES.

Espresso	$2.50
Cappuccino	$3.75
Latte	$4.00

RATING.

COFFEE	OVERALL
4.25 / 5	4.25 / 5

Oslo Williamsburg

133 Roebling Street, Brooklyn, NY 11211 | **Williamsburg** ·······································

A strong sense of community pervades this popular Williamsburg meeting spot, where hipster parents can often be seen grabbing after-school treats with their kids. Oslo is a decidedly social scene, where old friends come to catch up at the communal table in the huge front window or hang out with their dogs on the front benches. Newspapers and magazines are provided if you just feel like reading and relaxing, and the wide, open space makes Oslo a perfect spot to do just that. The coffee is a house blend, roasted nearby, and lattes here are particularly lovely.

OPEN.

Mon-Fri.   7:00am - 7:00pm
Sat-Sun.   8:00am - 7:00pm

OVERVIEW.

Category
Multi-independent
Owner
JD Merget and Kathy Merget
First opened
2002

COFFEE & EQUIPMENT.

Roaster
Oslo
Machine
La Marzocco Strada MP
Grinder
Mazzer Luigi
Bulk brewer
Fetco

Other locations
Bedford Avenue / East 75th Street

PRICES.

Filter / Drip	$1.50
Espresso	$2.50
Cappuccino	$3.25
Latte	$3.25

FOOD.

An assortment of cookies and muffins
from Blue Sky as well as croissants
from Ceci Cela Patisserie.

CONTACT.

(718) 782-0332
www.oslocoffee.com
info@oslocoffee.com
Subway L (Bedford Ave)

RATING.

COFFEE
4.25 / 5

OVERALL
4.00 / 5

Second Stop Cafe

524 Lorimer Street, Brooklyn, NY 11211 | **Williamsburg** ....

OPEN.

Mon-Fri.	7:00am - 9:00pm
Sat-Sun.	8:00am - 9:00pm

Definitely a hot spot for the computer-toting mobile workforce, this shop is a low-key, relaxing place to grab a cup and plow through some work. The space is bright, with sunshine streaming through ample windows into the front room, or down the back is another, quieter room for contemplation. This café is cozy in that Williamsburg kind of way, with a rustic, aged wooden interior, mismatched tables and artwork, as well as a warm, small-town vibe. All the food and baked goods are prepared fresh on site using homegrown herbs and local cheeses, and fresh juices are also available. A variety of single origins are offered on drip for those who wish to refine their palettes.

FOOD.

A full menu of breakfast offerings, sandwiches and salads, with a juice bar and lots of vegetarian and vegan options.

CONTACT.

(718) 486-6850
Subway L (Lorimer St) or G (Metropolitan Ave)

OVERVIEW.

Category
Independent
Owner
Paul Degruccio, Rosemarie Mangione and Craig Kafton
First opened
2009

COFFEE & EQUIPMENT.

Roaster
Dallis Bros Coffee
Machine
La Marzocco Linea, 2 groups
Grinder
Bunn, Ditting
Bulk brewer
Fetco

PRICES.

Filter / Drip	$2.25
Espresso	$2.25
Cappuccino	$3.75
Latte	$4.00

RATING.

COFFEE 3.75 / 5	
OVERALL 4.00 / 5	

Tar Pit

135 Woodpoint Road, Brooklyn, NY 11211 | Williamsburg ....

OPEN.

Mon-Fri.	7:00am - 7:00pm
Sat.	9:00am - 7:00pm
Sun.	9:00am - 5:00pm

Coming here is a little bit like visiting your grandmother's living room - if your grandmother was into cutting-edge coffee technology. Tucked away on a quiet block in Williamsburg, Tar Pit has an exceedingly relaxed and hospitable vibe. The small space, designed by co-owner Lauren Kidder, is decorated with antique clocks and light fixtures, as well as a welcoming floral couch. The baristas here are adept and unpretentious, using Kitten Coffee roasted in nearby Bed-Stuy to make top-notch espresso and creamy lattes. Come by during the summer for regular block parties, or for a cold-brewed iced coffee made with a Kyoto tower that looks like it could be part of a Rube Goldberg machine.

FOOD.

Baked goods from Champs Bakery and Checkmate To Your Cupcake.

CONTACT.

(347) 352-3552
www.tarpitcafe.com
Subway L (Graham Ave)

OVERVIEW.

Category
Independent
Owner
Lauren Kidder and Kerry Sano
First opened
2011

COFFEE & EQUIPMENT.

Roaster
Kitten Coffee
Machine
La Marzocco Firenze
Grinder
Rio
Bulk brewer
Bunn

PRICES.

Filter / Drip	$1.50
Espresso	$2.50
Cappuccino	$3.75
Latte	$4.00

RATING.

COFFEE
3.75 / 5

OVERALL
3.75 / 5

Toby's Estate

125 North 6th Street, Brooklyn, NY 11211 | **Williamsburg** ....

This first US outpost of the Australian-based roaster is without a doubt one of the top coffee destinations in New York. Head roaster Deaton Pigot travels the world tasting beans at origin, roasts the beans at this Williamsburg site in full view, then tastes the coffee you're about to drink in the cupping room. This hands-on approach ensures the single-origin pourovers are worth their higher price tags. The espresso is equally exceptional and if you're in the mood for something milky, order a flat white, the latte's stronger Australian sister, and the shop's signature espresso drink. The Toby's baristas are excellent, meticulously crafting each beverage no matter how long the line gets. Vintage general-store goods decorate the space, which is vast yet cozy, sophisticated and distinctive. There's plenty of space to sit down and sure, you could pull out your laptop and get some work done, but to do so would be akin to texting in church. Instead, give yourself a moment to take in the sacred beverage before you and soak up some sun from the enormous front windows.

Williamsburg

OPEN.
Mon-Fri. 7:00am - 7:00pm
Sat-Sun. 8:00am - 8:00pm

OVERVIEW.
Category
Chain
Owner
Toby Smith, Adam Boyd
and Amber Jacobsen
First opened
2012

COFFEE & EQUIPMENT.
Roaster
Toby's Estate
Machine
La Marzocco Strada EP
Grinder
Mazzer Robur E

PRICES.
Filter / Drip	Market price, varies
Espresso	$2.75
Cappuccino	$3.50
Latte	$4.25

FOOD.
A menu of housemade breakfast and
lunch dishes to match the excellent
coffee. Australian Tim Tam cookies and
pastries from Balthazar Bakery,
Ovenly Bakery and Piemonte are
also available.

CONTACT.
(347) 457-6160
www.tobysestate.com
email-us@tobysestate.com
Subway L (Bedford Ave)

RATING.
COFFEE 4.75 / 5
OVERALL 4.75 / 5

Variety Coffee & Tea

368 Graham Avenue, Brooklyn, NY 11211 | **Williamsburg** ································

OPEN.
Mon-Sun.   7:00am - 9:00pm

Variety's moniker is by no means arbitrary, as this wonderful neighborhood find combines a catalogue of virtues into a single concept. The café is as much a cool and quiet place to share a conversation as it is to comfortably nest and tap away at your laptop for a while, and the design of the space pleasingly combines Williamsburg ramshackle-chic with industrial exposed lightbulbs and a polished wooden bar. The freshly baked goods such as banana chocolate-chip loaf are equally as good as the Stumptown espresso. With a relaxed vibe and late hours, Variety is a versatile home for all your coffee needs.

FOOD.

Baked goods from neighborhood bakeries include muffins and loaves from Blue Sky, croissants from Ceci Cela and pastries from This Chick Bakes.

CONTACT.

(347) 599-2351
www.varietynyc.com
Subway L (Graham Ave) or G (Metropolitan Ave)

OVERVIEW.

Category
Multi-independent
Owner
Gavin Compton
First opened
2008

COFFEE & EQUIPMENT.

Roaster
Stumptown Coffee Roasters
Machine
La Marzocco Linea, 3 groups
Grinder
Mazzer Robur E

PRICES.

Filter / Drip	$1.50
Espresso	$2.50
Cappuccino	$3.50
Latte	$3.50

Other locations
145 Driggs Avenue / Miller's Tavern

RATING.

COFFEE
4.00 / 5

OVERALL
4.00 / 5

Greenpoint & Queens

Growing in popularity, the neighborhoods of Astoria, Long Island City and Greenpoint are hubs of culture, history and lots of good food. Greenpoint adjoins Williamsburg on the other side of McCarren Park and, although quiet, is full of innovative eateries and shops. Walk over Pulaski Bridge to Long Island City and explore a burgeoning part of Queens where lots of new restaurants, MoMA's contemporary art affiliate PS1 and a thriving creative community can be found. Astoria boasts a diverse cultural mix that includes Italian, Jewish and Greek communities.

Café Grumpy Greenpoint

193 Meserole Avenue, Brooklyn, NY 11222 | **Greenpoint** ....

With super friendly baristas, exceptional coffee and a bright, comfortable space, there's nothing remotely grumpy about Café Grumpy. Grumpy's coffee is roasted fresh at this location, its baked goods (all inventively delicious) are prepared at a bakery in lower Manhattan and everything is distributed fresh across the city to all four lovely Grumpy cafés. This is the largest of the four venues and the only one to offer wifi and allow computers, making it a truly delightful place to do some work or get distracted by the sunshine. The menu of single origins and espresso drinks is detailed and exciting, baristas are always happy to help and the case of gourmet muffins, loaves and scones just begs to be explored.

OPEN.

Mon-Thu.	7:00am - 7:00pm
Fri.	7:00am - 8:00pm
Sat.	8:00am - 8:00pm
Sun.	8:00am - 7:00pm

OVERVIEW.

Category
Multi-independent
Owner
Chris Timbrell and Caroline Bell
First opened
2005

COFFEE & EQUIPMENT.

Roaster
Café Grumpy
Machine
Synesso Cyncra, 2 groups
Grinder
Mazzer Robur E x 2, Mazzer Kony,
Ditting

Other locations
Park Slope / Chelsea / Essex Street

PRICES.

Filter / Drip	$2.75
Espresso	$2.75
Cappuccino	$3.75
Latte	$4.00

FOOD.

An array of fresh baked goods made at the Café Grumpy bakery on Essex Street in Manhattan.

CONTACT.

(718) 349-7623
www.cafegrumpy.com
cafegrumpy@gmail.com
Subway G (Nassau Ave)

RATING.

COFFEE 4.75 / 5	🌰🌰🌰🌰🌰
OVERALL 4.50 / 5	★★★★✬

Champion Coffee

1108 Manhattan Avenue, Brooklyn, NY 11222 | Greenpoint ....

OPEN.
Mon-Sun. 7:00am - 8:00pm

A small but powerful coffee bar at the far end of Greenpoint's Manhattan Avenue, Champion Coffee makes for a particularly lovely destination when the weather is fine and the garden is open out the back. The coffee menu is comprised of a variety of delicious espresso-based drinks made using a custom blend by local roaster Oslo and a beautiful Faema E61 machine. Croissants, muffins and fresh sandwiches round out the offer at this quiet little gem of a café.

FOOD.
Sandwiches, salads and baked goods from local purveyors such as Marquette and Blue Sky.

CONTACT.
(718) 383-5195
www.championcoffee.net
championcoffee@gmail.com
Subway G (Greenpoint Ave)

OVERVIEW.
Category
Independent
Owner
Talitha Whidbee
First opened
2006

COFFEE & EQUIPMENT.
Roaster
Custom blend by Oslo
Machine
Faema E61
Grinder
Rio

PRICES.
Filter / Drip	Americano: $2.25
Espresso	$2.25
Cappuccino	$3.25
Latte	$3.25

RATING.

COFFEE	
4.00 / 5	🫘🫘🫘🫘🫘
OVERALL	
3.75 / 5	★★★⯨☆

149

Cup

978 Lorimer Street, Brooklyn, NY 11222 | **Greenpoint** ....

OPEN.

Mon-Fri.	6:30am - 8:00pm
Sat-Sun.	7:30am - 8:00pm

This tiny, sun-soaked coffee bar is a little piece of perpetual spring in Greenpoint. The small number of seats here means locals are commonly sighted carrying vibrantly colored takeout cups around the neighborhood, sipping away on tiresome commutes or ambling about McCarren Park. There is a cheerfulness to every aspect of Cup, as the baristas will happily make guests a flat white or other drink on request, and the cute little lending library is a charming touch. In the summer, order a "cococano", an Americano made with coconut water, for something a little different; it's both immensely refreshing and, apparently, a great hangover cure.

FOOD.

The café features a small selection of baked goods from Balthazar, Champs and Love Bites.

CONTACT.

(646) 265-6494
www.cuponnorman.com
cuponnorman@gmail.com
Subway G (Nassau Ave)

OVERVIEW.

Category
Independent
Owner
Bianca and Jeremy Leroux
First opened
2009

COFFEE & EQUIPMENT.

Roaster
Plowshares
Machine
Expobar EB-61, 2 groups
Grinder
Mazzer Luigi, Bunn
Bulk brewer
Bunn

PRICES.

Filter / Drip	$2.00
Espresso	$2.25
Cappuccino	$3.25
Latte	$3.50

RATING.

COFFEE
3.75 / 5

OVERALL
3.75 / 5

Five Leaves

18 Bedford Avenue, Brooklyn, NY 11222 | Greenpoint ....

OPEN.
Mon-Fri.   8:00am - 1:00am

This New American bistro boasts a keen focus on quality coffee and is one of the best in a new wave of eateries that are aiming to craft quality coffee to match the caliber of their food. Five Leaves is packed on the weekends, with brunching locals and foodies hovering around the quaint corner, but during the week this venue is a little more sedate. If you don't want to brave the line or sit down and enjoy a full meal, grab a cup to go at the coffee takeout window and enjoy a wander around the neighborhood.

FOOD.
New American cuisine, with brunch on the weekends and pastries from Ceci Cela.

CONTACT.
(718) 383-5345
www.fiveleavesny.com
info@fiveleavesny.com
Subway G (Nassau Ave)

OVERVIEW.
Category
Independent
Owner
Jud Mongell and Kathy Mecham
First opened
2008

COFFEE & EQUIPMENT.
Roaster
Stumptown Coffee Roasters
Machine
La Marzocco
Grinder
Mazzer

PRICES.
Filter / Drip	Americano: $2.25
Espresso	$2.25
Cappuccino	$3.25
Latte	$3.50

RATING.

COFFEE
4.25 / 5

OVERALL
4.25 / 5

Milk & Roses

1110 Manhattan Avenue, Brooklyn, NY 11222 | **Greenpoint** ....

OPEN.

Sun-Thu.	8:00am - 11:00pm
Fri-Sat.	8:00am - midnight

A romantic spot at what feels like the edge of the world (although it is only the edge of Brooklyn), this quiet café is a special little secret out here in Greenpoint. Milk & Roses has a decidedly European atmosphere - dark, comfortable and almost mysterious in its hushed grandeur. The walls are lined with books, a collection the owner and his wife have acquired over time, and a piano sits modestly, waiting for the evening to come on Tuesdays, Thursdays and the weekends, when a pianist plays through the night. The espresso is soft and mild in flavor, and the Italian food is delicious and well priced. When the weather is obliging, venture into the back garden for some al fresco dining.

FOOD.

Italian sandwiches, salads, pastries and small bites.

CONTACT.

(718) 389-0160
milkandrosesbistro@gmail.com
Subway G (Greenpoint Ave)

OVERVIEW.

Category
Independent
Owner
Tomasso Mazzoni
First opened
2010

COFFEE & EQUIPMENT.

Roaster
Miscela D'oro
Machine
GrandPrix DiFormula, 2 groups
Grinder
GrandPrix

PRICES.

Filter / Drip	Americano: $2.25
Espresso	$2.25
Cappuccino	$3.00
Latte	$3.50

RATING.

COFFEE
4.00 / 5

OVERALL
4.25 / 5

The Queens Kickshaw

40-17 Broadway, Queens, NY 11103 | **Astoria** ....

If you're not into crowds, visit this table-service restaurant in Queens on a weekday morning when it's relaxed and not yet at capacity. Once you're here, stay all day - the place will transform from a seriously coffee-centric morning stop to a gourmet grilled cheese lunch spot and again into a low-key bar with an extensive beer list in the evening. 24-hour cold brewed coffee is also available on tap throughout the day. It's hard to go wrong with any of the menu's artisanal grilled cheese options, but the gouda with jalapeño and guava jam on brioche is particularly excellent.

OPEN.

Mon-Fri.	7:30am - 1:00am
Sat-Sun.	9:00am - 1:00am

OVERVIEW.

Category
Independent
Owner
Ben Sandler and Jennifer Lim
First opened
2011

COFFEE & EQUIPMENT.

Roaster
Coffee Labs Roasters
Machine
La Marzocco MP, 3 groups
Grinder
La Marzocco Volcano, Mazzer Major,
Ditting

PRICES.

Filter / Drip	$2.50
Espresso	$2.25
Cappuccino	$3.50
Latte	$3.75

FOOD.

The pastries are from Balthazar while the gourmet menu of inventive grilled cheese sandwiches, salads and soups is prepared in house.

CONTACT.

(718) 777-0913
thequeenskickshaw.com
info@thequeenskickshaw.com
Subway E, M, R (Steinway St)

RATING.

COFFEE
4.25 / 5

OVERALL
4.50 / 5

Sweetleaf

10-93 Jackson Avenue, Queens, NY 11101 | **Long Island City** ....

Sweetleaf is as genuine as it is delicious. The owners and baristas at this elegantly worn-in café really care about good service, endeavoring to make drink suggestions and helping customers learn about coffee and brewing methods as they pull delightfully flavorful shots. A tiny, stylish record room in the back allows customers to play something from the Sweetleaf vinyl library (or bring your own if you so choose), while the bright front room is a great place to watch the bakers whip up treats through a window into the kitchen. If you've got the time, order a pourover at the bar, take in a coffee lesson and enjoy what promises to be a special experience.

OPEN.

Mon-Fri.	7:00am - 7:00pm
Sat.	8:00am - 7:00pm
Sun.	9:00am - 6:00pm

OVERVIEW.

Category
Independent
Owner
Rich Nieto and Freddy Arundel
First opened
2008

COFFEE & EQUIPMENT.

Roaster
Stumptown Coffee Roasters,
Verve Coffee Roasters
Machine
La Marzocco Strada EP, 2 groups
Grinder
Mazzer
Bulk brewer
Bunn

Other locations
Williamsburg

PRICES.

Filter / Drip	$2.00
Espresso	$2.75
Cappuccino	$3.50
Latte	$3.50

FOOD.

A menu of gourmet housemade baked goods.

CONTACT.

(917) 832-6726
www.sweetleaflic.com
Subway G (21st St)

RATING.

COFFEE 4.50 / 5	🫘 🫘 🫘 🫘 🫘
OVERALL 4.50 / 5	★ ★ ★ ★ ½

Upright Coffee

860 Manhattan Avenue, Brooklyn, NY 11222 | Greenpoint ....

OPEN.

Mon-Fri.	7:00am - 8:00pm
Sat.	8:00am - 8:00pm
Sun.	8:00am - 6:00pm

A gem of a coffee shop hidden away in Greenpoint, Upright balances seriousness with neighborhood amiability. The streamlined menu of Brooklyn Roasting Company espresso drinks routinely impresses and this minimal approach extends to the space, which contains only a few stools, hence the shop's name. Although its compact size might not give you cause to linger, the care and friendliness of the baristas at Upright Coffee will.

FOOD.
Pastries from Ceci Cela Patisserie.

CONTACT.
(718) 215-9910
uprightcoffee.com
info@uprightcoffee.com
Subway G (Nassau Ave)

OVERVIEW.
Category
Independent
Owner
Michael Medovoy and Daniel Neumann
First opened
2011

COFFEE & EQUIPMENT.
Roaster
Brooklyn Roasting Company
Machine
La Marzocco Linea
Grinder
Mazzer
Bulk brewer
Fetco

PRICES.

Filter / Drip	$2.00
Espresso	$2.50
Cappuccino	$3.50
Latte	$3.75

RATING.

COFFEE 4.00 / 5

OVERALL 3.75 / 5

VIVA LA
REUSE
REVOLUTION

THE FIRST BARISTA STANDARD REUSABLE CUP

keep
cup

BETTER & BETTER
KEEPCUP.COM

Coffee Glossary

Acidity: one of the principal categories used by professional tasters to determine the quality of a coffee or blend along with flavor, aroma and body. Usually refers to the pleasant tartness of a fine coffee and not the pH level.

Aeropress: a hand-powered device for brewing coffee that forces water through ground coffee at high pressure.

Affogato: a coffee-based dessert - usually a scoop of vanilla ice cream topped with a shot of hot espresso.

Americano, Caffè Americano: an espresso with hot water added.

Arabica, Coffea arabica: the earliest cultivated species of coffee tree and still the most widely grown. Arabica produces approximately 70% of the world's coffee and is dramatically superior in cup quality to other principal commercial coffee species such as Coffea canephora or Robusta.

Aroma: the way a coffee smells. Aroma is one of the principal categories used by professional tasters to determine the quality of a particular coffee or blend. Examples of aromas include earthy, spicy, floral and nutty.

Blend: a combination of coffees from different countries and regions that achieve a taste no single coffee can offer alone.

Body: the heaviness, thickness or relative weight of coffee on the tongue when tasted. Body is one of the principal categories used by professional tasters to determine the quality of a coffee or blend.

Brew group: in an espresso machine, the brew group contains the portafilter and group head. It needs to be heated in order to brew espresso.

Brew temperature: is dependent on the extraction method. For filter and French press, water should be just below boiling, and the consensus is that espresso should be brewed with water at 88-120°C.

Brew time: the time it takes for an espresso to pour from a portafilter spout - one of the key indicators of a good espresso shot. The guideline for an espresso brew time is 25-30 seconds.

Café au lait: one-third drip coffee with two-thirds hot frothed milk.

Café con leche: a traditional Spanish coffee consisting of espresso served with scalded milk.

Café mocha or mocha: similar to a caffè latte, but with added chocolate syrup or powder.

Caffeine: an odourless, bitter alkaloid responsible for the stimulating effect of coffee and tea.

Cappuccino: one-third espresso, one-third steamed milk and one-third frothed milk. A traditional Italian cappuccino is 4.5oz, but in the USA they are usually larger. Often topped with powdered chocolate or cinnamon.

Cherry: a term used to refer to the fruit of the coffee plant, each of which contains two coffee beans.

Cortado: a traditional Spanish coffee made with a shot of espresso and a dash of warm milk to reduce acidity.

Crema: the pale brown foam on the surface of an espresso, created by the dispersion of gases in liquid at high pressure. A sign of a well-extracted shot.

Cupping: a method by which professional tasters perform sensory evaluation of coffee beans. Water is poured over ground beans and the coffee is left to stand for a few minutes to allow extraction. The taster smells the coffee, then slurps it from a spoon or directly from the cup. The grounds remain within the liquid, so tasters often spit it out after allowing the flavor, body and acidity to register in the mouth.

Dispersion screen: an essential part of the brew group that ensures the correct dispersion of brewing water over the portafilter and filter basket.

Dosage: the amount of ground coffee used for each brewing method. For espresso, dosage should be 7g per 1.5oz shot.

Doppio: a double espresso, or three to six ounces of straight espresso.

Drip or filter method: a brewing method that allows hot water to settle through a bed of ground coffee, either with or without a filter paper.

Espresso: the basis for the majority of coffee beverages in coffee shops, made by forcing hot water at high pressure through 7g of finely ground coffee to produce 1.5oz of extracted beverage.

Extraction: the act of turning water into brewed coffee or espresso by allowing coffee to sit in hot water for a period of time or forcing hot water through ground coffee.

Filter basket: sits in the portafilter and holds a bed of ground coffee. The basket has a multitude of tiny holes in the bottom to allow the extracted beverage to seep through and pour into a cup.

Filter method: any brewing method in which water filters through a bed of ground coffee. Most commonly used to describe drip method brewers that use a paper filter to separate grounds from brewed coffee.

Coffee Glossary cont.

Flat white: an espresso-based beverage hailing from Australia and New Zealand made with a double shot of espresso and finely steamed milk (or microfoam). Typically served as an 8oz drink, a flat white is similar to a traditional Italian cappuccino and is often served with latte art.

Flavor: one of the principal categories used by professional tasters to determine the quality of a coffee or blend. Flavor refers to the taste and notes such as citrus, nutty, earthy and exotic, which describe the coffee.

French press, plunger pot, cafétiere: brewing method that separates spent grounds from brewed coffee by pressing them to the bottom of the brewing receptacle with a mesh plunger.

Froth / foam: as milk is steamed using a steaming wand, air is introduced into the liquid, resulting in the production of froth. As the steam agitates and heats the milk, it increases in volume and the wand tip is moved towards the surface. This draws air at high velocity into the milk, creating the foam or froth. Steamed milk and froth should be poured, not spooned, into the cup.

Green coffee (green beans): unroasted coffee.

Grind: the extent to which whole coffee beans are ground, a factor that will play a significant role in determining the resulting coffee brewed from it.

A coarse grind should be used for a brewing method where the grounds will sit in the water for a period of time. A very fine grind is suited to high-speed brewing or extraction methods such as espresso.

Grouphead: the part of the brew group containing the locking connector for the portafilter and the dispersion screen. An integral part of the espresso machine, the grouphead helps to maintain temperature stability in the machine, essential for producing a perfect shot.

Latte or caffè latte: a shot of espresso combined with about three times as much hot milk, topped with foamed milk.

Latte art: the pattern or design created by pouring steamed milk into a shot of espresso. Only properly steamed milk will hold its form, and latte art is a good sign of a skilled barista.

Long black: made by pulling a double shot of espresso over hot water. Similar to an Americano, but different in that it retains the crema from the espresso and has a stronger flavor.

Macchiato: a serving of espresso "stained" with a small quantity of hot frothed milk (espresso macchiato) or a moderately tall (8oz) glass of hot frothed milk "stained" with espresso (latte macchiato).

Macrofoam or dry foam: the stiff foam containing large bubbles that is created when steaming milk for a cappuccino.

Microfoam: the ideal texture of steamed milk for espresso-based coffee drinks, particularly those with latte art. Microfoam is made using a steam wand on an espresso machine and typically has much smaller bubbles than macrofoam.

Moka pot or stovetop: a manual method of making strong coffee. Often brewed on a stove, this type of coffee pot forces hot water through a bed of coffee using the pressure of steam and produces a strong, condensed shot of coffee.

Over extracted: a term used to describe coffee with a bitter or burnt taste, usually the result of exposing hot water to ground coffee for too long. To make the perfect coffee, water should be introduced for a set amount of time, depending on how coarsely or finely the coffee beans have been ground.

Percolation: any method of coffee brewing in which hot water percolates or filters down through a bed of ground coffee. The pumping percolator utilises the power of boiling water to force water up a tube and over a bed of ground coffee.

Piccolo: a version of a caffè latte served in a macchiato glass consisting of a shot of espresso topped with milk and foam.

Pod: a self-contained, pre-ground, pre-pressed puck of ground coffee, usually sold individually wrapped inside a perforated paper filter. The pod is used in a specific type of coffee machine and is designed for ease of use.

Pourover: a method of drip coffee in which a thin, steady stream of water is poured slowly over a filter cone filled with ground coffee.

Portafilter (groupo): the device that combines a filter basket and a handle that is designed to be quickly attached to an espresso machine. Water is forced through the portafilter and espresso pours from the spout underneath.

Puck: after a shot of espresso has been brewed, the bed of coffee grounds forms a hard, compressed object that resembles a hockey puck. Also referred to as a spent puck.

Red eye: a shot of espresso fortified with drip coffee.

Ristretto: a restricted shot made using the same dose of ground coffee as a double espresso, but with only about 1.5oz (or less) of water, poured in the normal brewing time of 25-30 seconds. The result is a richer and more intense beverage.

Coffee Glossary cont.

Roast: the method by which green coffee is heated in order to produce coffee beans for consumption. Roasting begins when the temperature inside the green bean reaches approximately 200°C (this varies between different varieties of beans). Caramelisation occurs as intense heat converts starches in the bean to simple sugars that begin to brown, giving the coffee bean a resulting brown colour.

Robusta, Coffea canephora: the next most cultivated coffee species after Coffea arabica, robusta produces about 30% of the world's coffee. Robusta is grown at lower altitudes than arabica and is a hardy, robust plant that can produce high yields. The flavor is often less refined and robusta has a much higher caffeine content than arabica.

Shot: a single unit of brewed espresso.

Single origin: coffee from a particular region or farm.

Steam wand: the visible external pipe found on most espresso machines that is used to froth and steam milk.

Siphon: a brewing method that uses two glass chambers and a direct heat source to create a fragrant, delicately flavored cup of coffee.

Tamp (tamping): the act of pressing and compacting a bed of loose ground coffee into the portafilter basket in preparation for brewing espresso. The harder the coffee is tamped, the tighter the puck and the harder it is to extract the coffee. If the coffee grounds are too loosely tamped, the water will flow through too quickly.

Under extracted: describes coffee that has not been exposed to water for long enough. The resulting brew is often weak and thin-bodied.

Whole bean coffee: coffee that has been roasted but not yet ground.

A-Z List of Coffee Venues

A-Z List of Coffee Venues cont.

www.natvia.com

New York is awesome!

Every cup of coffee
has been divine.
Been to some of
the most fantastic
coffee joints ever.

Yesterday, Blue
Bottle. Today, Grumpy.
Tomorrow, Joe
West Village.

Love it!

And lots of love to
Natvia too! The 100%
Natural Sweetener.
Favourite of baristas
around the world.

PS. Don't forget to keep
a look out on www.
sendmetovienna.com for
the inside scoop for the
next city in the Natvia
Send Me To series.

Serve
Good Karma